TRUMP
TALKING

UNAUTHORISED

TRUMP
TALKING

The Donald,
in his own words

UNAUTHORISED

Al Cimino

ROBINSON

ROBINSON

First published in Great Britain in 2016 by Robinson

13 5 7 9 8 6 4 2

A CIP catalogue record for this book
is available from the British Library.

ISBN: 978-1-47213-915-3 (paperback)

Typeset in Minion Pro by SX Composing DTP, Rayleigh, Essex
Printed and bound in Great Britain by CPI Group (UK) Ltd, Croydon CR0 4YY

Papers used by Robinson are from well-managed forests and
other responsible sources

MIX
Paper from
responsible sources
FSC® C104740

Robinson
is an imprint of
Little, Brown Book Group
Carmelite House
50 Victoria Embankment
London EC4Y 0DZ

An Hachette UK Company
www.hachette.co.uk
www.littlebrown.co.uk

Contents

Introduction

The Donald

It was Donald Trump's first wife, former Czech Olympic skier Ivana Zelníčková, who first dubbed her husband 'The Donald'. It was a mistake, she explained.

'As most people know, English isn't my first language, in fact it's my fourth,' she told *The Washington Post*. 'When I came to live in New York, I really had to learn the language from the beginning almost. Some things come easily, some things don't. And for whatever reason, probably because I was going at my usual turbo speed, I started putting "The" in front of most people's names. Yes, you know the outcome – "The Donald" just slipped off the tongue, and now it seems to be making its ways to the political history books.'

The Donald said he had 'no choice' but to accept the nickname.

'I don't mind that it stuck,' he said. 'I think it's an endearment.'

Indeed, in an article in *Spy* magazine in 1989 that first made reference to her habit of putting 'the' in front of people's names, Ivana calls her husband 'The Don', which, for fans of *The Godfather*, could have more sinister connotations. Nevertheless, The Donald embraced his sobriquet. The opening sentence of his 1997 book *The Art of the Comeback* reads: 'It's usually fun being "The Donald".'

Long after they were divorced, Ivana laid claim to the epithet. She filed an application to trademark it, so she could exploit its commercial possibilities. She wanted to use the name, 'The Donald', for a cocktail and for a line of clothing. The Donald does not drink and is known as a snappy dresser. It was also to be used for a fragrance.

In her defence, Ivana said 'The Donald' in question was actually her son, Donald, Jr., not his dad. Donald, Sr. was not happy with this.

'I don't think Donny wants to be referred to as "The Donald". And for good reason. I would very much like not to be referred to as "The Donald". I would like to do without it,' he said, happily contradicting his earlier statement.

Ivana played a cameo role in the 1996 movie *The First Wives Club*, delivering the memorable line, 'Remember girls: don't get mad, get everything.'

With 'The Donald' she didn't. He, as always, threatened to sue. In the end, both backed down, so now 'The Donald' belongs to the world.

1

Trumpery

Donald Trump had made his name a brand. The name appears on every one of his buildings – including the ones he does not own any more. Seventeen buildings in New York City bear his name, though he owns only a handful of them. Tourist snap selfies beneath the oversize 'TRUMP' sign at 40 Wall Street.

'I put my name on buildings because it sells better,' he told *Larry King Live* in 1999. 'It's just a better product. But I get more than other people. So when I put my name on it, people say: "Oh, gee, he put his name on it."'

There have been objections. Howls of protest went up when 'TRUMP' appeared in 20-foot-6-inch-high letters on the top of the Trump International Hotel & Tower in Chicago in 2014. Donald was unapologetic.

'As time passes, it'll be like the Hollywood sign,' he told the *Chicago Tribune*'s architect critic Blair Kamin.

◆

'Nothing wrong with ego,' he told *Playboy* in March 1990. Then there is the much quoted: 'Show me someone without an ego, and I'll show you a loser.' The Donald is unequivocal: 'Every successful person has a very large ego.' So you need a very large sign.

He also told the magazine: 'The show is Trump. And it is sold-out performances everywhere.'

◆

Trump was concerned about his image early on in his career in real estate. He asked the *Village Voice* in 1979: 'What do people say about me? Do they say I'm loyal? Do they say I work hard?' His virtues must be broadcast. On that he was insistent.

'I really value my reputation and I don't hesitate to sue,' he added.

◆

And you have to pump up the brand. 'I play to people's fantasies,' he admitted in his bestselling 1987 book *The Art of the Deal*. 'People may not always think big themselves, but they can still get very excited by those who do. That's why a little hyperbole never hurts. People want to believe that something is the biggest and the greatest and the most spectacular.'

That is because: 'In a lot of ways it is easier to do things on a large scale. It is easier to build a skyscraper in Manhattan than it is to buy a bungalow in the Bronx. For one thing, it takes just as much time to close a big deal as it does to close a small deal. You will endure as much stress and aggravation; you will have all the same headaches and problems.'

But maybe that was hyperbole.

The following year, The Donald made a deal with Ted Turner to make *Don Trump: The Movie*.

'I want a very good-looking guy to play me,' he said.

Again, when he heard that HBO was planning a film based on his battles in Atlantic City in 2003, he told the *New York Post*: 'I want to be played by a very handsome, very brilliant person.'

In 1990, he asked a reporter from *Vanity Fair*: 'Did you see that *The New York Times* said I looked like Robert Redford?' The article was from 1976.

Vanity Fair were to run their own profile of him.

'How long is your article?' he asked. 'Is it a cover?'

Always deft when handling the press, he told a reporter from *Time* magazine, as they looked down from his helicopter flying into Atlantic City: 'I'll tell you, it's Big Business. If there is one word to describe Atlantic City, it's Big Business. Or two words: Big Business.' The Donald only counts in billions.

◆

Although already a millionaire several times over and hurtling towards the corporate bankruptcy of the Taj Mahal Casino – later, the Trump Taj Mahal – Donald, a boy from Queens, wanted to portray himself as the man of the people. 'There are two publics as far as I'm concerned. The real public and then there's the New York society horseshit,' he told *Vanity Fair*. 'The real public has always liked Donald Trump. The real public feels that Donald Trump is going through Trump-bashing. When I go out now, forget about it. I'm mobbed. It's bedlam.'

◆

Emerging from the Taj Mahal bankruptcy and his first marriage, he was eager to be seen as the devil-may-care playboy. 'You know, it really doesn't matter what they write as long as you've got a young and beautiful piece of ass,' he told *Esquire* in 1991.

◆

It was difficult to leave all that glitz behind. 'People say the '80s are dead, all the luxury, the extravagance. I say, "What?" Am I supposed to change my taste because it's a new decade? That's bullshit,' he told *Playboy* in May 1997.

◆

But Donald felt misunderstood. 'The press portrays me as a wild flamethrower,' he told *The New Yorker*. 'In actuality, I think I'm much different from that. I think I'm totally inaccurately portrayed.' He is, of course, a shrinking violet.

———◆———

'The fact is that I don't like publicity. I absolutely hate doing interviews,' he revealed to *People* magazine, in an interview.

———◆———

That's because the attention brings with it problems. He ran into neighbourhood opposition in 1999 when building Trump World Tower across from the United Nations building in New York City.

'If someone else was building it, there would be no opposition,' he told *The Miami Herald*. 'I build the highest-end buildings in New York. They sell for the most per square foot of anybody. That makes me happy, but because of the high profile, I tend to bring out the worst in people.'

Besides, as he explained to Associated Press: 'It's clear on the face that the few opponents, and they are few, aren't even able to read the simplest of English.' No wonder The Donald is sceptical about the United Nations. Indeed, he suggested to a US Senate subcommittee that the UN move to the site of the World Trade Center, so the current site could be redeveloped – making millions.

He had similar problems when developing the Trump National Golf Club in Westchester, New York.

'I think being Trump is a huge asset and it's a huge liability,' he told the *New York Observer* in 1999. 'I think that if I were a developer up in Westchester, I think probably it would have been a little less controversial, probably a lot less controversial. But it wouldn't have been the quality that it is.'

The business model is everything. 'I have made the tough decisions, always with an eye toward the bottom line,' he told LGBT-interest magazine *The Advocate* in 2000. 'Perhaps it's time America was run like a business.' Was he already preparing for a hostile takeover?

You see, money talks. 'That's why the banks love me. They love my reputation,' he told *The New York Times* on 28 March 2004.

The Trump brand expanded into TV courtesy of *The Apprentice* USA – co-producer and host, Donald J. Trump – putting rivals squarely in their place.

'Other rich people don't do commercials because no one asks them. It's just like *The Apprentice*. I can't tell you how many of my rich friends are dying, dying to have me put them on that show,' he told *The New York Times* on 11 August 2004.

He was, of course, the secret of its success.

'There is something crazy, hot, a phenomenon out there about me, but I'm not sure I can define it and I'm not sure I want to. How do you think *The Apprentice* would have done if I wasn't a part of it? There are a lot of imitators now and we'll see how they'll do, but I think they'll crash and burn,' he told the newspaper in September.

Naturally, The Donald was lured into fame. 'There's something very seductive about being a television star,' he said in the teleconference at the beginning of the third season, also announcing a possible theatrical spin-off.

'Every producer on Broadway wants to get involved with us,' he said. 'I think it would be a smash.'

'I can't help it that I'm a celebrity,' he told *USA Today*. 'What am I going to do, hide under a stone?'

'If I get my name in the paper, if people pay attention, that's what matters,' he confided to Gwenda Blair, author of *Donald Trump: Master Apprentice*.

◆

Branding is everything.

'I think the brand is huge,' he was quoted saying in *TrumpNation: The Art of Being The Donald* by Timothy O'Brian. 'What is it about me that gets Larry King his highest ratings?'

Similarly, he took credit for the viewing figures of the Republican debate in August 2015: 'Who do you think they're watching? Jeb Bush? Huh? I don't think so.'

And it all came about by accident.

'A lot of people build a brand and they study it very carefully and every move is calculated. My moves are not calculated. My moves are totally uncalculated,' he went on.

'If you asked Babe Ruth how he hit home runs, he was unable to tell you. I do things by instinct,' he told *The New York Times*.

◆

The brand is The Donald and The Donald is the brand. 'My brand became more famous as I became more famous, and more opportunities presented themselves,' he said in an interview on Amazon.com in 2007.

And the brand is about being a winner. Back in 1988, he launched a board game called Trump: The Game. He even appeared in the TV commercial. The advertising slogan on the box and for the commercial was: 'My new game is

Trump: The Game'. And the slogan: 'It's not whether you win or lose, it's whether you win'.

Nearly thirty years later the game is a collector's item.

◆

'I don't like to lose,' he told *The New York Times* on 7 August 1983. Later he said: 'I'll do nearly anything within legal bounds to win.'

◆

In *TrumpNation: The Art of Being The Donald*, Timothy O'Brian quotes him ranting: 'If you don't win you can't get away with it. And I win, I win, I always win. In the end, I always win, whether it's in golf, whether it's in tennis, whether it's in life, I just always win. And I tell people I always win, because I do.'

Maybe The Donald has mellowed. In August 2015, he told CNN: 'I do whine because I want to win, and I'm not happy about not winning, and I am a whiner, and I keep whining and whining until I win.'

◆

On *The Apprentice,* The Donald gets to pick who is a winner or a loser. He tried to copyright the catchphrase. 'Every time you walk down the street people are screaming, "You're fired!" It's in case I ever decide to do something with it,' he told the *New York Post* in March 2004.

Plainly, there is poetry in his soul. He told the *San Francisco Chronicle*: "'You're fired!': There's a beauty in those two words. When you utter those words, there's very little that can be said. There's a succinctness to those words.'

◆

The reality is very different. 'I don't like firing people,' he told the *Boston Herald*. 'It's not a pleasant thing and it's sad… In some cases, it's a terrible, terrible situation for the person who gets fired, how strongly they take it. So it's not something that any rational or sane person can love doing, but it also happens to be a fact of life in business.'

Elsewhere, he said: 'Generally I like other people to fire, because it's always a lousy task.'

◆

However in extreme cases, Donald is prepared to do it. He fired Marvin Roffman, a financial analyst from Philadelphia, after he said that the Trump Taj Mahal was in for a rough ride.

'I'd do it again,' Trump told Marie Brenner of *Vanity Fair*.

Things then got nasty with Roffman suing Trump for defamation of character.

Brenner was then told by one of the lawyers involved in the case: 'Donald is a believer in the big-lie theory. If you say something again and again, people will believe you.'

When Brenner put that to Trump, he said: 'One of my lawyers said that. I think if one of my lawyers said that, I'd like to know who it is, because I'd fire his ass. I'd like to find out who the scumbag is!'

The Roffman suit was settled out of court.

On Fox News, Trump recalled firing Oxana Fedorova, the 2002 Miss Universe, who was from Russia: 'She did a terrible job as Miss Universe. She was lazy and every other thing you can think of. And I enjoyed firing her.'

Fedorova claimed to have given up the crown for personal reasons, mainly to finish her law degree. She went on to have a successful career on Russian TV.

The Trump brand has extended well beyond the United States. During his campaign to become the Republican presidential candidate, Donald Trump became an unexpected columnist on the Aberdeen *Press and Journal*. Although there are no votes for him in Scotland, he has a golf course on the Aberdeenshire coast.

'When I first arrived on the scene in Aberdeen, the people of Scotland were testing me to see how serious I was – just like the citizens of the United States have done about my race for the White House,' he wrote. The rookie pundit also confidently claimed that 'Scotland has already been won, and so will the United States.'

However, plucky fisherman Michael Forbes continued to stand in his way, refusing to sell his farm to the tycoon.

'I'll never ever sell to Trump,' he told the *New York Daily News*. 'He's pissed me off now.'

Trump offered him $750,000 for the land and a job for life at his new resort.

'He can take his money and shove it up his arse,' said the doughty Scotsman, 'I don't care about his money.'

In January 2016, Trump threatened to pull his £700 million worth of investment when Scotland sought to ban him entering the UK after he talked of banning Muslims from the US. A petition garnered more than 568,000 signatures. He also threatened to cut his losses after failing to block plans for an offshore wind farm that would spoil the view.

His column did not go down well with the residents of Aberdeen.

'It would anger me more if there was any element of truth to it,' said Hamish Gibson, a student at the city's ancient university and creator of a movement to tell the former *Apprentice* boss he had been fired and scrap the column.

'Most people reading the article would not believe it,' he said. 'It isn't just inaccurate but offensive to people in the Northeast. The idea he has in any way "won" in Scotland is preposterous.'

2

Tycoonery

On 14 May 1990, the cover story of *Forbes* magazine asked: 'How Much Is Donald Trump Worth?' The magazine's answer was about $500 million – though only the year before *Forbes* had put the figure at $1.7 billion. Donald complained that the magazine had undervalued assets such as the Plaza Hotel, the Trump Shuttle, and 'seventy-eight acres of land I own on Manhattan's Upper West Side', among others.

'Who can say what these one-of-a-kind assets are worth until they're put on the market?' said Trump. 'Certainly not a mediocre reporter from *Forbes*...'

———◆———

According to Donald, the reason for *Forbes*' attack was 'yacht envy'. The *Trump Princess* measured 282 feet, while publisher Malcolm Forbes' boat was around a relatively paltry 150 feet. Also there was an incident at the Oak Room Bar in Trump's Plaza Hotel when Forbes' underage guest was refused a seat by the management.

Donald claimed full credit for this. He told *Vanity Fair*: 'You know the story about me and Malcolm Forbes, when I kicked him out of the Plaza hotel? No? Well, I did. You'll read all about it in my new book.'

Later, he was filled with contrition.

'I think I'm giving up the game of who's got the best boat,' he said, opining: 'The second-greatest day of a man's life is the day he buys a yacht, but the greatest day of a man's life is the day he sells it.'

When Trump ran into financial problems in 1991, he sold the *Trump Princess* to the Saudi billionaire Prince Al-Waleed bin Talal.

Nevertheless, a little residual 'yacht envy' remained. In 1996, he told the *Philadelphia Inquirer*: 'I've always wanted a boat bigger than the Queen's.' The 412-foot Royal Yacht *Britannia* was decommissioned the following year. The Queen has now downsized: the royal barge *Gloriana* commissioned for her diamond jubilee in 2012 is just 94 feet long. So Donald is in with a chance.

'Yacht envy' resurfaced in April 2013, when he could not help tweeting: 'I've always been a fan of Steve Jobs, especially after watching Apple stock collapse w/out him – but the yacht he built is truly ugly.'

It's tough being a tycoon. 'Look at these contracts,' he told *The New Yorker* in May 1997. 'I get these to sign every day. I've signed hundreds of these. Here's a contract for $2.2 million. It's a building that isn't even opened yet. It's eighty-three per cent sold, and nobody even knows it's there. For each contract, I need to sign twenty-two times, and if you think that's easy.'

All the buyers want his signature. When he had someone else who works for him signing, the buyers got angry.

'I told myself, "You know, these people are paying a million eight, a million seven, two million nine, four million one – for those kinds of numbers, I'll sign the f**king contract." I understand. F**k it. It's just more work.'

◆

Don't go thinking he has been feather-bedded.

'My whole life really has been a "no" and I fought through it,' Trump told an NBC-sponsored town hall meeting at Atkinson, New Hampshire, in October 2015. 'It has not been easy for me; it has not been easy for me. And you know I started off in Brooklyn, my father gave me a small loan of a million dollars.'

Trump quickly pointed out that 'a million dollars isn't very much compared to what I've built.'

Later he inherited part of the more than $200 million portfolio his father left.

◆

'I'm not a schmuck,' he told the *Chicago Tribune* in 1989. 'Even if the world goes to hell in a handbasket, I won't lose a penny.'

The newspaper went on to point out why. The Trump Taj Mahal in Atlantic City cost $725 million to build, but Donald spent only $50 million. The other $675 million was financed in uncollaterized junk bonds. The Taj was at the centre of three of Trump's corporate bankruptcies, which he sailed through practically unscathed.

Everything was above board, of course.

'I know people that are making a tremendous amount of money and paying virtually no tax, and I think it's unfair,' he said during the second Republican debate in September 2015.

◆

Fortune begets fortune. Donald told *The Washington Post* in July 2015: 'Let's say I was worth $10. People would say, 'Who the [expletive] are you?' You understand? They know my statement. Fortune. My book, *The Art of the Deal*, based on my fortune. If I didn't make a fortune, who the [expletive] is going to buy *The Art of the Deal*? That's why they watched *The Apprentice*, because of my great success.'

◆

There have been some tough times, though. He told *New York* magazine in August 1994: 'Hey, look, I had a cold spell from 1990 to '91. I was beat up in business and in my personal life.

But you learn that you're either the toughest, meanest piece of shit in the world or you just crawl into a corner, put your finger in your mouth, and say, "I want to go home." You never know until you're under pressure how you're gonna react. Guys that I thought were tough were nothin'.'

However, he conceded ten years earlier: 'Let me tell you something about the rich. They have a very low threshold for pain.'

Naturally, Donald is the ultimate masochist.

'I have an unlimited appetite for pain,' he told *The New York Times* in June 2001. 'That's a secret to my success. I just can't give up.'

But Donald is no cissy. 'I learned about toughness in a very tough business,' he said. 'It's much easier to sell an apartment to Johnny Carson or Steven Spielberg for $4 million than it is to collect a couple of dollars of rent in Brooklyn.'

People find it easy to traduce Donald.

'People think I'm a gambler,' he complained in *Time* magazine in April 1990. 'I've never gambled in my life. To me, a gambler is someone who plays slot machines. I prefer to own slot machines. It's a very good business being the house.'

The house, like Donald, will always be the winner.

'I like the casino business. I like the scale, which is huge, I like the glamour, and most of all, I like the cash flow.'

'How much have I made off the casinos?' he was quoted saying in *Master Apprentice*. 'Off the record, a lot.'

However, in April 2004, he was quoted in the *Pittsburgh Post-Gazette* saying: 'My life is like a game of poker.' But that's OK too, if you own the casino.

Besides Donald is not quite as much of a player as he thinks. When he brought out Trump: The Game, a Vegas poker player took out full-page newspaper ads offering $1 million to play the game against him. Donald declined.

'Part of being a winner is knowing when is enough is enough,' he says in Jamie Grant's *The Donald Trump Handbook*. 'Sometimes you have to give up the fight and walk away. Move on to something that's more productive.'

It was not gambling – or not – that counts, but selling.

'I know how to sell. Selling is life,' he told *Sports Illustrated* in February 1984. 'You can have the greatest singer in the world, but if nobody knows who he is, he'll never have the opportunity to sing.'

And later: 'There are singers in the world with voices as good as Frank Sinatra's, but they're singing in their garages because no one has ever heard of them. You need to generate interest, and you need to create excitement.'

———◆———

But, of course, every good salesman must be a little economical with the truth.

'Have you ever exaggerated in statements about your properties?' one lawyer asked him in a Florida court on 28 July 2015.

'I think everyone does,' Mr Trump replied.

'Does that mean that sometimes you'll inflate the value of your properties in your statements?' asked the lawyer.

'Not beyond reason,' he answered.

———◆———

When he announced his bid for the Republican presidential nomination in June 2015, he claimed he was worth nearly $9 billion.

'I'm proud of my net worth, I've done an amazing job... The total is $8,737,540,000 US. I'm not doing that to brag, because, you know what, I don't have to brag.'

However, the notoriously left-wing *Forbes* magazine said at the time his net worth was less than half that, at just $4.1 billion, while Bloomberg put his net worth at $2.9 billion.

But The Donald does not bother with the nickels and dimes. In his account of one of his four business bankruptcies, he claimed his debts had reached $9 billion. Challenged by the flagrantly liberal *The New York Times*, he said: 'Frankly, whether it's $9 billion or $3.6 billion – I don't think makes any difference to anybody if they hear the story.'

As he explained in a tweet in September 2014: 'Money was never a big motivation for me, except as a way to keep score. The real excitement is playing the game.'

◆

On the darker side, he said: 'Everything in life to me is a psychological game, a series of challenges you either meet or don't.'

◆

As he fought his way to the top, The Donald developed these thoughts into a philosophy.

'For many years I've said that if someone screws you, screw them back,' he said. 'When somebody hurts you, just go after them as viciously and as violently as you can.'

In *USA Today* in 2000, it was: 'If someone screws you, screw them back harder.'

Then in 2004, when you would not have thought pennies were an issue, he told *Esquire*: 'Fighting for the last penny is a very good philosophy to have.'

The Washington Times in January 2012 got: 'It's important to focus on the solution, not the problem.'

Other gems include: 'Your money should be at work at all times'; 'Sometimes your best investments are the ones you don't make'; and 'Buy companies only when you understand what they do.'

———◆———

Donald's view of life was summed up in his attitude to the contestants on *The Apprentice*: 'They arrive in a limo at Trump Tower, and when they're fired, they leave in a cab. That's how life is.' Not on foot, then.

———◆———

The philosophy extended to the nurturing of children.

'When you're rich, you can have as many kids as you want,' he said. 'Being rich makes it easier to have kids.'

Indeed, Donald found it easy enough.

'I want five children, like in my own family, because with five, then I will know that one will be guaranteed to turn out like me,' he said.

Nevertheless, business comes before parenthood.

'The hardest thing for me about raising kids has been finding the time,' he told *New York* magazine. 'I know friends who leave their business so they can spend more time with their children, and I say, "Gimme a break!"'

Donald has indeed succeeded in having five children, by three different mothers.

———◆———

It paid off in the end, when announcing he was running for the nomination, he said: 'I don't need anybody's money. It's nice. I don't need anybody's money. I'm using my own money. I'm not using the lobbyists. I'm not using donors. I don't care. I'm really rich, I'll show you that in a second. And by the way, I'm not even saying that in a braggadocios... that's the kind of thinking you need for this country.'

But money brings with it paranoia. 'It's wonderful to believe in the power of positive thinking and all, but they're after your job. They're all after your position. They're all after your money. I've never seen a great businessman who wasn't a little bit paranoid,' he told *USA Today*, 12 March 2001.

'We hunt for pleasure. So you have to really be a little bit paranoid. There are so many stories about people who have been decimated by people they trusted,' The Donald said in *The Hoya*, Georgetown University's twice-weekly newspaper, on 4 December 2001. Perhaps he was anticipating a Dick Cheney moment.

'Be paranoid. Now that sounds terrible, but you have to realize that people, sadly, sadly, are very vicious. You think we're so different from the lions in the jungle?' he told the

Kansas City Star, in February 2000. Being paranoid doesn't mean that they're not out to get you, it seems.

———◆———

Trump negotiated for fifteen months with the city of New Rochelle for rights to develop Davids' Island. The price was $13 million but Trump offered $12,999,999.99.

'Being superstitious, I thought I might make it a little bit complicated,' he said.

'It's always good to do things nice and complicated so that nobody can figure it out,' he told *The New Yorker* in May 1997.

———◆———

The Donald is naturally house-proud. 'While I can't honestly say I need an 80-foot living room, I do get a kick out of having one,' he said.

Then there is the library.

'We have to buy a lot of books,' he said. 'I really respect books. … We have great art too.'

There are hand-carved marble columns. The walls are lined in Italian gold onyx and the ceiling mouldings are 23-carat gold. The ceiling is painted with various mythological heroes.

'There has never been anything like this built in 400 years,' he said. 'If this were on the ceiling of the Sistine Chapel, it would be very much in place in terms of quality. This is really what you call talent, more talent than the schmucks who go around throwing paint on the canvas.'

And he really knows about art. In 1989, he told *Time* magazine: 'I can sit down with the most sophisticated people in the arts in New York and get along fabulously with them. If I want to, I can convince them that I know as much about something as they do, and I don't.'

Giving a reporter from Associated Press a tour, he said: 'This is called luxury, this is Trump luxury. One of the most luxurious buildings in the world.... You see why Trump is Trump.'

His apartment has a bulletproof sauna and a lead-lined towel closet with a false rear wall for quick escapes. 'That's for when they come in with the machine guns,' he told *Life* magazine.

Outraged at being offered royal palm trees for one of his golf clubs for $300, rather than the usual $5,000, he told the *Palm Beach Post*: 'Somebody once sent me flowers – roses. The roses were $300. How could a tree that grows fifty feet up in the air cost only $300?'

When Trump opened Club Mar-a-Lago, one member wanted his $25,000 membership fee back because he said he was promised that celebrities would be around for him to mingle with, and two that attended on opening day – Tony Bennett and Lee Majors – were not high-calibre enough for him:

'This guy is a loser who did this to create publicity for himself and because he needs his money back. He doesn't like Tony Bennett. He wanted Madonna. Can you believe it?' Donald told *USA Today*.

Does Madonna play golf? I can't imagine a loser being out for publicity and that's for winners only.

The key to The Donald's business strategy in the early days seems to be shameless overcharging. On 1 July 1986, *The New York Times* reported a snippet from the court files of the United State Football League anti-trust case against the National Football league. In it, The Donald gave lucid insight into his business practices. In 1984, he told a meeting of the USFL: 'When I build something for somebody, I always add $50 million or $60 million onto the price. My guys come in, they say it's going to cost $75 million. I say it's going to cost $125 million. Basically I did a lousy job. But they think I did a great job.'

He had polished his technique since then.

———◆———

'Once you've hit the big time as a billionaire, you should convince business travelers on a one-hour flight from New York to Washington that it's worth paying more to have a golden toilet,' he's quoted saying in *TrumpNation*.

———◆———

At a lunch in the Washington Press Club in May 2014, Donald was asked how he relaxes. 'I build buildings,' he said.

3

Mein Trumpf

According to Ivana, Donald would read *My New Order*, the collected speeches of Hitler from 1918 to 1939, which he kept in a cabinet by the bed. Donald claimed that his friend Martin Davis, head of Paramount, gave him a copy, not of *My New Order* but of *Mein Kampf* – 'and he's a Jew.' Davis insisted that it was *My New Order* and he was not Jewish.

'If I had these speeches, and I am not saying that I do, I would never read them,' Trump told *Vanity Fair* in 1990.

Ivana also said that her husband's cousin and employee, John Walter, 'clicks his heels and says, "Heil Hitler",' when visiting Trump's office, though this was possibly a family joke.

It has to be said that Donald's oratorical style owes little to Adolf.

◆

Addressing a group of Republicans at Warburg College in Waverly, Iowa, he asked: 'Did you notice that baby was crying through half of the speech and I didn't get angry? Not once. Did you notice that? That baby was driving me crazy. I didn't get angry once because I didn't want to insult the parents for not taking the kid out of the room?'

Adolf would never have put up with a baby crying.

——◆——

Not that Donald had any political ambitions back when he was married to Ivana. 'I have no intention of running for president,' he told *Time* in September 1987.

'I don't want to be president. I'm 100 per cent sure. I'd change my mind only if I saw this country continue to go down the tubes,' he told *Playboy* in March 1990.

He went on: 'I would hate to think that people blame me for the problems of the world. Yet people come to me and say, "Why do you allow homelessness in the cities?" as if I control the situation. I am not somebody seeking office.'

Adding: 'Well, if I ever ran for office, I'd do better as a Democrat than as a Republican – and that's not because I'd be more liberal, because I'm conservative. But the working guy would elect me. He likes me.'

——◆——

By the year 2000, he had changed his mind for the best of reasons, telling *Fortune* magazine: 'It's very possible that I could be the first presidential candidate to run and make money on it.'

After all: 'Cash is king, and that's one of the beauties of the casino business.'

However, when deciding not to run in 2000, he said: 'I'm not prepared to throw [my money] away. I'd rather go to Atlantic City and take a bet on the tables.' If you own the casino, you can't lose.

But in 2016, he rued: 'I'm giving up hundreds of millions of dollars to do this. I'm giving up a prime-time television show… I'm in it to win it.' Is he playing the Lottery, then?

Later, in *Unleash The Billionaire Within* by Esmonde Holowaty, he said: 'I've always told people that to be successful you have to enjoy what you're doing and right now I really enjoy what I'm doing. I'm having too much fun with my life. Why would I want to do something else? Why would I want to run for governor?' Only governor? What happened? He got tired of million-dollar deals and beauty pageants?

But by 2011, Donald had a positive programme. 'We build a school, we build a road, they blow up the school, we build another school, we build another road, they blow them up, we build again – in the meantime we can't get a f**king school in Brooklyn,' he told an adoring crowd in the Treasure Island Hotel in Las Vegas.

He had, however, been working up a political agenda in the meantime – and it was going to be tough. 'I think if this country gets any kinder or gentler, it's literally going to cease to exist,' he said in 1990. '…people are virtually afraid to say, "I want the death penalty." Well, I want it. Where has this country gone when you're not supposed to put in a grave the son of a bitch who robbed, beat, murdered and threw a ninety-year-old woman off the building?'

He said he hated seeing the country go to hell and being laughed at by the rest of the world.

'In order to bring law and order back into our cities, we need the death penalty and authority given back to the police.'

That worked out well, then. In certain cases, the police have brought the death penalty back to the cities – and no one is laughing.

By the year 2000, he was asking key questions that should have been resolved fifty-five years earlier: 'Would it have been civilized to put Hitler in prison? No – it would have been an affront to civilization…. My only complaint is that lethal injection is too comfortable a way to go.'

Plainly, executing criminals does have an effect.

'A hundred per cent of the people who are executed never commit another crime,' he said. That's for sure.

More guns are the answer. Despite the continued plague of school shootings, he asserts: 'The government has no business dictating what types of firearms good, honest people are allowed to own.'

Not only that, a conceal-carry permit, a state licence to carry a conceal firearm, should be valid in all fifty states.

'A driver's licence works in every state, so it's common sense that a concealed-carry permit should work in every state. If we can do that for driving – which is a privilege, not a right – then surely we can do that for concealed carry, which is a right, not a privilege.'

He has a concealed-carry permit himself.

The same *Trump: Make America Great Again!* website dealing with the Second Amendment right to keep and bear arms states: 'Our mental health system is broken. It needs to be fixed. Too many politicians have ignored this problem for too long.'

Asked if he had ever considered psychotherapy, he said: 'No. I've never felt even close to needing it. I haven't ever felt that I was out of control. I keep busy. I don't have time to think about my problems.'

He had his doubts in other quarters, though.

'I'm starting to think that there is something seriously wrong with President Obama's mental health. Why won't he stop the flights? Psycho!' he tweeted on 16 October 2014 after two Dallas healthcare workers came down with Ebola.

Appearing later on *The Steve Malzberg Show*, he refused to back down. 'Can anybody be that incompetent?' he asked. 'There's something wrong, there's something going on.'

But then he believed everything Obama had done in his entire presidency was wrong.

'Every decision this country has made is wrong,' Trump said. 'Everything's wrong. Everything is going wrong for the United States. When was the last time you heard something good about the United States? You don't hear it. China just took over as the great economic power... this was unthinkable.'

———◆———

This was because Obama was dumb.

'I heard he was a terrible student, terrible. How does a bad student go to Columbia and then to Harvard?' Trump told the Associated Press. 'How do you get into Harvard if you are not a good student? Maybe that's right, maybe that's wrong, but I don't know why he doesn't release his records.'

Obama graduated from Columbia University in New York in 1983 with a degree in political science after transfer-ring from Occidental College in California. He went on to

Harvard Law School, where he graduated *magna cum laude* in 1991 and was the first African-American president of the *Harvard Law Review.*

Donald himself attended the Wharton School of Business, 'the hardest school to get in … the best school. It's like super genius stuff,' he claimed.

'I was a really good student at the best school. I'm like a smart guy, OK,' he said on talkshow *The View* in 2011.

The New York Times questioned whether he even graduated. Nobody has seen the records.

'Who knows what's in the deepest part of my mind?' he told a reporter from BuzzFeed in February 2014. And in a moment of Rumsfeldian enlightenment that year, The Donald tweeted: 'The more you know, the more you realize how much you don't know.'

As well as being enigmatic, The Donald had other advantages: 'I can be a killer and a nice guy. You have to be everything. You have to be strong. You have to be sweet. You have to be ruthless. And I don't think any of it can be learned. Either you have it or you don't. And that is why most kids can get straight A's in school but fail in life.'

So when it came to Obama: 'The last guy he wants to run against is Donald Trump.'

———◆———

That challenge was made in 2011. But The Donald did not run for president.

'I never said I was running,' he explained. 'I don't know what happened to Mitt Romney. It looked like he was going to do fine. I was leading in every poll. I was doing great.'

———◆———

It was a missed opportunity. In 2011, The Donald declared: 'If I decide to run, you'll have the great pleasure of voting for the man that will easily go down as the greatest president in the history of the United States. Me. Donald John Trump.'

———◆———

When he did eventually decide to run in 2015, he told the *Des Moines Register*: 'I'm the most successful person ever to run for the presidency, by far. Nobody's ever been more successful than me. I'm the most successful person ever to run.' Not George Washington who beat the British, then? Or Dwight D. Eisenhower, supreme commander of the Allied force in Western Europe that defeated Hitler?

———◆———

Donald Trump has been quoted on different occasions saying that Jimmy Carter, George W. Bush, and Barack Obama
were each: 'The worst president ever.' And he is determined
to do something about that.

'Politicians are all talk and no action' is one of his favourite
lines. However, at a hearing over a failed Florida real estate
project, he said: 'I'm no different from a politician running
for office.' This was in July 2015, the month after he
announced he was running.

'I'm tired of politicians being president, because I see the
lousy job they do, and I'm just tired of it. And I think a lot
of other people are,' he told *Larry King Live* in October 1999.
Who was he thinking should replace them? Ballerinas?
Artists? Authors? No, silly me. Businessmen.

But Donald dipped his toe in the water way back in the days
when he was expanding his father's real estate empire:
'When you need zone changes, you're political. ... You
know, I'll support the Democrats, the Republicans, whatever the hell I have to support.'

Donald Trump was a Republican from 1987 to 1999, from
2009 to 2011, and 2012 onwards. He was a Democrat before

1987 and from 2001 to 2009. He was with the Reform Party from 1999 to 2001 and an Independent from 2011 to 2012.

———◆———

'I will be the greatest jobs president God ever created,' he said when he announced that he was running for the nomination in June 2015. Which is ironic as his catchphrase on *The Apprentice* was: 'You're fired.'

He said famously: 'I could never have imagined that firing 67 people on national television would actually make me more popular, especially with the younger generation.' Imagine how popular he would be if he fired 67 million. Would that be the Hispanics — sorry, Mexicans — the Muslims and the African Americans? That's Obama taken care of, then.

———◆———

Donald has never been good with employment figures. When he announced he was running for president on 16 June 2015, he said: 'Our real unemployment is anywhere from 18 to 20 percent. Don't believe the 5.6. Don't believe.'

The Bureau of Labor Statistics' figure at the time was 5.5 per cent. Then on 20 August, he told *Time* magazine: 'Our real unemployment rate is 42 per cent.'

The implication is that the federal government is cooking the books and 5 per cent was a 'phony number'. To calculate the unemployment rate, the agency simply divides the number of people who are out of work by the total work force. But then, the Bureau of Labor Statistics were, he believed, a 'bunch of clowns, bunch of real clowns'.

The Washington Post's Fact Checker traced the 42 per cent back to a column by David Stockman, who once served as President Ronald Reagan's budget director, where he took the number of working hours actually recorded and divided it by the potential working hours of everyone in America aged between sixteen and sixty-eight, giving 'a real unemployment rate of 42.9 percent'. However, Stockman admitted that this included 'non-working wives, students, the disabled, early retirees and coupon clippers … drifters, grifters, welfare cheats, bums and people between jobs, enrolled in training programs, on sabbaticals and much else.'

People voluntarily working part-time, rearing children, attending school or college, being ill or disabled, or who are rich enough to take early retirement, are lazy bums, apparently.

———◆———

'Look, my whole campaign is about honesty,' The Donald told *The Washington Post*, 9 December 2015. So that sort of reporting may soon be a thing of the past. Speaking at a rally in Fort Worth, Texas on 26 February 2016, Trump pledged if elected president to 'open up our libel laws so when [newspapers] write purposely negative stories … we can sue them and make lots of money'.

The move, he said, would mean that 'when *The New York Times* or *The Washington Post* writes a hit piece, we can sue them'.

This would require some slight adjustment to the First Amendment, which states that 'Congress shall make no law … abridging the freedom of speech, or of the press.' It's been in place for 225 years now. To change it requires a two-thirds majority in both houses of Congress and ratification by thirty-eight of the fifty states. This could take some time. The ratification process for the last amendment to the Constitution, the twenty-seventh, took a record-breaking 202 years, seven months and twelve days.

———◆———

The Second Amendment 'the right of the people to keep and bear arms' – must be maintained at all costs, though

'It is so important that we maintain the Second Amendment and we maintain it strongly,' Trump told Breitbart News. 'And one of the main reasons is because we good people, the upstanding people, follow laws and norms but the bad ones don't. So if the Second Amendment weren't there to protect our rights and someone tampered with them, the good people would be affected but the bad people wouldn't care – they couldn't care less.

'Paris has virtually the most restrictive laws that exist anywhere, and you look at the slaughter at *Charlie Hebdo*, and that's what it was – it was a slaughter in which the people never had a chance. And I made the statement then that if people had guns in that room the outcome would have been a hell-of-a-lot better than it ended up being, where they were just slaughtered at will …

'If the people so violently shot down in Paris had guns, at least they would have had a fighting chance.'

Mao Tse-tung said: 'Political power grows out of the barrel of a gun.' Or more accurately: 'Every Communist must grasp the truth: political power grows out of the barrel of a gun.' Communist, did you grasp that, Donald?

And the Second Amendment, of course, says: 'A well regulated Militia, being necessary to the security of a free State, the right of the people to keep and bear arms, shall not be infringed.'

◆

There is another lesson to be learned. After the massacre in Paris in November 2015, The Donald said: 'When Paris happened, everyone started saying, "We want Trump!" The polls came in, 60 per cent, 70 per cent, 72 per cent. This is 72 percent with 17 people running. Now we're down to 6, we got rid of all these people. It's so great. It's so great.'

◆

Interviewed by Robert Costa from *The Washington Post* for a piece headlined: LISTENING TO DONALD TRUMP SWEAR AND TALK POLITICS ON HIS PRIVATE PLANE in July 2015, The Donald said: 'This is a movement. It's a very different movement than I think you've ever seen before.'

Movement might well be the appropriate word for it.

◆

There is no doubt that The Donald is an original thinker, though. In March 2015, he bragged: 'The line of "Make America great again", the phrase, that was mine, I came up with it about a year ago, and I kept using it, and everybody's using it, they are all loving it. I don't know I guess I should copyright it, maybe I have copyrighted it.'

In fact, Donald's hero Ronald Reagan used 'Let's make America great again' as his campaign slogan thirty-five years earlier.

Nevertheless, in July, The Donald was still insisting: 'This campaign is about making America great again. I copyrighted it.' Sorry, this should read "Making America great again" ©Donald J. Trump, 2015.

—◆—

'The worst things in history have happened when people stop thinking for themselves, especially when they allow themselves to be influenced by negative people. That's what gives rise to dictators. Avoid that at all costs. Stop it first on a personal level, and you will have contributed to world sanity as well as your own,' he wrote in both his books *Real Estate 101* and *Think Like A Champion*. Wise words, Donald.

—◆—

Campaigning in Buffalo, upstate New York, he said of the events of 9/11: 'It's very close to my heart because I was down there, and I watched our police and our firemen down at 7-Eleven, down at the World Trade Center right after it came down, and I saw the greatest people I've ever seen in action.'

We all admire those who work long hours in convenience stores.

4

Trumpadour

Donald Trump is often ridiculed for his perma-tan and his improbable hair, styled in what is now widely known as a Trumpadour – or even Trump-adore. However, his 2004 book *Trump: How to Get Rich* had a chapter called 'The Art of the Hair' where he proudly quotes *New York* magazine saying that he had 'perfected the art of the pompad-over' and *The New York Times* calling it 'an elaborate structure best left to an architecture critic'. Undeterred, The Donald goes on: 'Personally, I think it looks good, but I've never said my hair was my strongest point.'

—◆—

The Donald is insistent: 'I do not wear a rug. My hair is one hundred per cent mine', adding, 'No animals have been harmed in the creation of my hairstyle.' It is hard to believe that his coiffure qualifies as hairstyle. One would have assumed that it had been blown that way by a malevolent wind. As he said himself in *The Art of the Deal* in 1987: 'Sometimes it pays to be a little wild.'

———◆———

'I get up, take a shower and wash my hair,' he told *Playboy* in 2004. 'Then I read the newspapers and watch the news on television, and slowly the hair dries. It takes about an hour. I don't use the blow dryer. Once it's dry I comb it. Once I have it the way I like it – even though nobody else likes it – I spray it and it's good for the day.' Unless the wind blows, that is.

———◆———

But then that's not a problem: 'The reason my hair looks so neat all the time is because I don't have to deal with the elements very often. I live in the building where I work. I take an elevator from my bedroom to my office. The rest of the time, I'm either in my stretch limousine, my private jet, my helicopter, or my private club in Palm Beach, Florida.'

If he is outside, on one of his golf courses, say, 'I protect my hair from overexposure by wearing a golf hat. It's also a way to avoid the paparazzi.' Or not – the golf hat always has the TRUMP logo on.

He considered changing his hairstyle for the second series of *The Apprentice*. 'But probably not,' he said, 'it seems to be working.'

———◆———

Discussing his hair with *San Jose Mercury News* in January 2004, he said: 'It's been good to me over the years. Maybe that's my problem.'

He admitted colouring his hair: 'Somehow, the color never looks great, but what the hell, I just don't like grey hair.'

That March, he told the *Philadelphia Inquirer*: 'I get more abuse on the hair. It's been this way since the time I was in high school. ... I don't like to change things. It seems to me to be working. Is it that bad?'

On an episode of *The Oprah Winfrey Show* broadcast on 8 April 2004: 'I actually had somebody come up to me who was interviewing me and said, "Well, what about the hair?" And then she just got off the chair and she just pulled my hair up. And she said, "It's real," and "I don't believe it."'

Then in 2011, Oprah offered to give his hair a makeover.

'What's the difference between a wet raccoon and Donald Trump's hair? A wet raccoon does not have seven billion f**king dollars in the bank,' he told the Comedy Central cable network at his celebrity Roast in 2011.

In an interview with *Rolling Stone* in 2011, he again explained his routine: 'OK, what I do is, wash it with Head and Shoulders. I don't dry it, though. I let it dry by itself. It takes about an hour. Then I read papers and things...

'OK, so I've done all that. I then comb my hair. Yes, I do use a comb.... Do I comb it forward? No, I don't comb it forward...'

He then pulled up the loose flap.

'I actually don't have a bad hairline. When you think about it, it's not bad. I mean, I get a lot of credit for combovers. But it's not really a combover. It's sort of a little bit forward and back. I've combed it the same way for years.'

———◆———

His hair became a battlefield. On 24 April 2013, he tweeted: 'As everybody knows, but the haters & losers refuse to acknowledge, I do not wear a "wig." My hair may not be perfect but it's mine.' That's taken a weight off my mind, though not, apparently, his.

———◆———

'I've been called out by everybody for the ALS ice bucket challenge. Homer Simpson, Mike Tyson, Vince McMahon ... I guess they want to see whether or not it's my real hair, which it is.' Miss Universe and Miss USA were dragooned into administering the ice bucket challenge on YouTube in 2014.

In June 2015, he told the *Des Moines Register* that people often asked him if he would do his hair differently if he was elected president. His reply was: 'I would probably comb my hair back. Why? Because this thing is too hard to comb. I wouldn't have time, because if I were in the White House, I'd be working my ass off.'

Or perhaps this was because his daughter Ivanka and his wife Melania often tell him he needs to act more 'presidential,' he said. What, with hair like that?

'I don't care if it's not presidential,' he said in March 2016. He was talking about businesses that were planning to move manufacturing outside the United States. 'I want Carrier not to leave our country. I want Nabisco not to leave our country. I want Ford not to leave our country.'

Fleeing already?

Out on the stump, he still had to reassure voters in South Carolina: 'I don't wear a toupee. It's my hair, I swear.' Nevertheless he had to invite a woman from the audience to run her fingers through it.

'Yes, I believe it is,' the woman said, assuring the crowd that it really was attached to his head.

Even so, the *Huffington Post* carried a cruel tweet that read: 'I can't trust someone as our president that has hair that looks like a guinea pig #DonaldTrump.'

5

Blowing Your Own Trumpet

In January 2016, Trump told a crowd: 'I could stand in the middle of Fifth Avenue and shoot somebody, and I wouldn't lose any voters.' He would certainly be one down, unless that is where he thinks Hillary still does her shopping.

———◆———

Donald is never shy about doling out advice: 'don't let the brevity of these passages prevent you from savoring the profundity of the advice you are about to receive.' That was from his book *How to Get Rich* in 2004. The paperback is 320 pages long. Brief it's not.

———◆———

But then Donald is not one to hide his light under a bushel.

'I'm intelligent. Some people would say I'm very, very, very intelligent,' he told *Fortune* magazine in April 2000.

Then he told *Time* magazine in April 2011: 'I am a really smart guy.'

By comparison, he said in Las Vegas: 'Our leaders are stupid. They are stupid people. It's just very, very sad.'

To ram home the message, he tweeted in May 2013: 'Sorry losers and haters, but my I.Q. is one of the highest – and you all know it! Please don't feel stupid or insecure. It's not your fault.' I guess I will just have to live with it, then.

'Vision is my best asset. I know what sells and I know what people want,' he told *Playboy* in March 1990. 'I don't dwell on the past.'

In 2014, he tweeted: 'I try to learn from the past, but I plan for the future by focusing exclusively on the present. That's where the fun is!'

Then there's: 'In life you have to rely on the past, and that's called history.'

Conversely, in July 2015, he told *The Washington Post*: 'I don't look forward or not look forward.' He looks sideways?

The secret of Donald's success is, apparently, lack of sleep.

'I tell my competitors who need eight or ten hours of sleep a night that they're at a major disadvantage,' he says.

'While everybody else is sleeping, I'm thinking, reading reports, statements. It's like living two lives. I'll have twice the amount of time most people have on Earth.'

There are a lot of things to have sleepless nights about.

'I don't sleep more than four hours a night... I'm a guy who lies awake at night and thinks and plots.'

Not only that: 'I rarely stop for lunch.'

Who does he think he is? Gordon Gekko?

So which one said: 'The point is, you can never be too greedy'? (Answer: The Donald.)

Walking along the streets of New York City in 1990, Donald noted that 'about twenty-five perfect strangers wave and shout, "Hi, Donald," and "How're you doing, Donald," and "Keep up the good work."'

This proved to Donald that the average working man or woman was a lot better adjusted and more secure than the 'supposedly successful' people who looked down from the penthouses.

Later he discovered this was a worldwide phenomenon. In Brazil, 'I was surprised and delighted that children came running up to me with pencils and paper yelling, "Mr Trump, Mr Trump."'

In May 1997, he told *New York* magazine: 'You want to know what total recognition is? I'll tell you how you

know you've got it. When the Nigerians on the street cor-
ners who don't speak a word of English, who have no clue,
who're selling watches for some guy in New Jersey – when
you walk by and those guys say, "Trump! Trump!" That's
total recognition.'

It had to be the hair, surely. They'd never seen anything
like it.

———◆———

As time went by, Donald began identifying with fellow
kooky tycoon Howard Hughes and his famous aversion to
germs, saying: 'I've always had very strong feelings about
cleanliness. I'm constantly washing my hands.'

Unfortunately, pressing the flesh is very much part of the
business if you're running for office, and Donald told *The
New Yorker* in May 1997: 'Know what? After shaking five
thousand hands, I think I'll go wash mine.'

He went further in 1999, telling NBC's *Later Today*: 'I'm
not a big fan of the handshake. I think it's barbaric. I mean,
they have medical reports all the time. Shaking hands, you
catch colds, you catch the flu, you catch this. You catch all
sorts of things. Who knows what you don't catch?'

Later he told the *Rivera Live* TV series: 'Clinton was
shaking hands with 500 or 600 people; he then got into the
back of the presidential limo, grabs a sandwich and he eats
it, and no problem. I wish I could be like that. I just can't.'

———◆———

So when Ebola struck he went right to the heart of the problem, tweeting: 'Something very important, and indeed society changing, may come out of the Ebola epidemic that will be a very good thing: NO SHAKING HANDS!' It played into his hands, as it were.

———◆———

'Stop the EBOLA patients from entering the US. Treat them, at the highest level, over there. THE UNITED STATES HAS ENOUGH PROBLEMS,' said another tweet. He also called for all infected American healthcare volunteers in West Africa to be barred from returning to the US. One can only assume that these heroes may want to shake hands with the next president of the United States.

———◆———

Then The Donald lent his medical expertise to the vexed field of vaccinations. 'No more massive injections. Tiny children are not horses – one vaccine at a time, over time,' he tweeted on 3 September 2014.

'I am being proven right about massive vaccinations – the doctors lied! Save our children & their future,' he tweeted again the same day.

The following day, he clarified: 'I'm not against vaccinations for your children, I'm against them in one massive dose. Spread them out over a period of time and autism will drop!'

'So many people who have children with autism have thanked me – amazing response. They know far better than fudged up reports!' he later trumped.

'I've seen people where they have a perfectly healthy child, and they go for vaccinations, and a month later, the child is no longer healthy,' he said in a TV debate with fellow GOP and neurosurgeon Dr Ben Carson. 'I think when you add all of these vaccinations together and then two months later the baby is so different then lots of different things have happened. I really – I've known cases.'

That added to the scientific debate, then.

Cancer is another matter. He told the *Milwaukee Journal Sentinel* in November 2003: 'I don't like talking about failure. I don't even like thinking about failure. You know, when people tell me there's this new food that causes cancer, I say, "Do me a favor: Don't even mention that word." I don't want to hear about any of that stuff.'

In his 2000 book *The America We Deserve*, Donald explained why he had the right to speak out on such matters: 'Because I've been successful, make money, get headlines, and have authored bestselling books, I have a better chance to make my ideas public than do people who are less well known.'

———◆———

If The Donald is not a medical man, perhaps he is an artist.

'Other people paint beautifully on canvas or write wonderful poetry. I like making deals, preferably big deals,' he said. 'Deals are my art form.'

———◆———

He told the *Toronto Star*: 'I look at things for the art sake and the beauty sake and the deal sake.' And *Playboy*: 'I do what I do out of pure enjoyment. Hopefully, nobody does it better. There's a beauty to making a great deal. It's my canvas and I like painting it.'

———◆———

And there are other comparisons. 'I've always felt that a lot of modern art is a con,' he said, 'and that the most successful painters are often better salesmen and promoters than they are artists.'

———◆———

He told the TV show *Wall Street Week with Fortune*: 'You know I just love real estate. It's tangible, it's solid, it's beautiful. It's artistic, from my standpoint, and I just love real estate.'

His talents aren't confined to the artistic: 'It is an ability to become an entrepreneur, a great athlete, a great writer. You're either born with it or you're not.'

He also tried his hand as a movie reviewer, saying: 'I went to the opening of *The Dark Knight Rises*, which is commonly known as "the Batman movie." And I'll tell you, it was really terrific.'

But there's always the money.

'My attitude is if somebody's willing to pay me $225,000 to make a speech, it seems stupid not to show up. You know why I'll do it? Because I don't think anyone's ever been paid that much,' he told *The New Yorker* in May 1997.

Then when he threatened to run for president in 2012, he told *Time*: 'I look very much forward to showing my financials, because they are huge.'

And when he announced he was running in 2016, he said. 'I'm really rich.' Not that there was anyone who didn't know.

But The Donald is adamant about self-promotion: 'If you don't tell people about your success, they probably won't know about it.'

—◆—

'Did you know that *New York Construction News* named Donald Trump the developer and owner of the year?' he told *Fortune* in April 2000.

—◆—

'I think the only difference between me and the other candidates is that I'm more honest and my women are more beautiful,' he said in Miami in 1999.

—◆—

'Some people cast shadows, and other people choose to live in those shadows,' he told *The New York Times* in September 2005. The man's a colossus.

—◆—

'You gotta say, I cover the gamut. Does the kid cover the gamut? Boy, it never ends. I mean, people have no idea. Cool life. You know, it's sort of a cool life,' he told *The New Yorker* in May 1997.

—◆—

'I nod, and it is done,' he said in *Esquire* in January 2004.

—◆—

He also told the crowd at the announcement of his candidature: 'I think I am a nice person. People who know me like me.' Are you sure, Donald? Perhaps you should ask fellow Republican Ted Cruz about that.

'I enjoy testing friendships,' he told *Playboy*. 'You can never tell until you test; the human species is interesting in that way.'

Back in 1989, he told *Time* magazine: 'Those who dislike me don't know me, and have never met me. My guess is that they dislike me out of jealousy.'

After all, he said: 'Who has done as much as I have? No one has done more in New York than me.'

He also said: 'I love to have enemies. I fight my enemies. I like beating my enemies to the ground.' And: 'My style of dealmaking is quite simple and straightforward. I just keep pushing and pushing and pushing to get what I'm after.'

It's all down to attitude.

'The mind can overcome any obstacle,' he told *The New York Times* in 1983. 'I never think of the negative.'

Four years later, he had modified his views: 'It's been said that I believe in the power of positive thinking. In fact, I believe in the power of negative thinking.'

But by 2005, he had become AC rather than DC: 'A lot of people sit down and discuss their lives, things like are they happy, but it's not like that with me. I don't think positively, I don't think negatively, I just think about the goal. But it's not like I sit down and write goals. I just do things.'

But then The Donald is not happy.

'I'm not the world's happiest person,' he told *New York* magazine in March 1990. I can feel the tears welling.

'I've had a lot of victories,' he told *People* in July 1990. 'I fight hard for victory, and I think I enjoy it as much as I ever did. But I realize that maybe new victories won't be the same as the first couple.'

But the thrill never dies. He told *Atlantic* in April 2013: 'I've done an incredible job.'

'I like the challenge and tell the story of the coal miner's son,' he told *Playboy*. 'The coal miner gets black-lung disease, his son gets it, then his son. If I had been the son of a coal miner, I would have left the damn mines. But most people don't have the imagination – or whatever – to leave their mine. They don't have "it."'

'It' being the spare $1 million given to them by their father.

———◆———

But you cannot say that The Donald did not know hardship in his youth.

'My father was successful, but it was a different kind of success,' he told *The Washington Post* in November 1984. 'I didn't grow up like this. When I played golf, I played at the public course. I'd go to the state park and wait four hours to tee off when I was fourteen.'

———◆———

There again, some sons are dogged by successful fathers.

'Look, I had friends whose fathers were very successful, and the fathers were jealous of the sons' success and tried to hurt them, keep them down, because they wanted to be the king,' Donald told *The New York Times*. 'My father was the exact opposite. He used to carry around articles [about me].'

Elsewhere, he said: 'I was always very much accepted by my father. He adored Donald Trump.'

Nice to know they were on first-name terms.

———◆———

'There's a big difference between creating wealth and being a member of the lucky sperm club,' he told *Inside Politics* in January 2000. Then again, he believed: 'Everything in life is luck.'

'When luck is on your side it is not the time to be modest or timid,' he said. But then nobody could accuse him of being either modest or timid.

'Some people call me lucky, but I know better,' he claimed in *Think Big*. It was because, he said: 'I am no stranger to working hard. I have done it all my life.'

———◆———

This is what makes him a man of the people. He told Brian Kilmeade on the morning news show *Fox & Friends*: 'The people that like me the best are the middle class and poor people. The rich people hate me, it's true! ... Because I think they're jealous, because I think they want to be famous.'

He also agreed with Kilmeade's assessment that he has a 'natural relationship with the blue-collar worker.'

———◆———

He does not like to play the proletarian card, though.

'For years, I watched politicians brag how poor they were, how poor their family is, how poor their grandparents were, and how their families have been losers for years and years. And, "Elect me, because I'm a loser,"' he told the *Contra Coast Times* in Walnut Creek, California, in January 2000.

———◆———

But he does have connections.

'When the Queen of England is over in this country,' The Donald told *Time* magazine, 'they call my office to find out if they can use the helicopter because it's the safest helicopter.'

Said vehicle was a ten-seat French Puma, which he bought for $2 million (he claims it was worth $10 million). It had TRUMP painted in large white letters on the black fuselage, and he used it to commute once a week between New York and Atlantic City.

And he had a head for heights.

'I don't think anything scares me. … My pilots are the best, and I pay whatever it takes. When it comes to pilots, doctors, accountants, I don't chisel.'

'I can never apologize for the truth,' Donald told Fox News in July 2015.

'This man is a pathological liar, he doesn't know the difference between truth and lies,' said Ted Cruz. 'Whatever lie he's telling at that minute he believes it.'

Indeed, The Donald did not apologize.

In February 2014, he told BuzzFeed: 'I do love provoking people.'

As a master of Twitter, he had the tools at his hand. In March 2014, he told an audience at the Washington Press Club: 'I have millions of followers. Millions. I don't do press releases any more. … It's like owning *The New York Times* without the lawsuits.'

He had already tweeted in October 2012: 'My twitter has become so powerful that I can actually make my enemies tell the truth.'

He uses it to speak out on all the big issues. 'I have never seen a thin person drinking Diet Coke,' he tweeted on 14 October 2012. The Donald is hardly sylphlike. And he can't blame it on the beer. Perhaps it was the bottle of Diet Coke that eagle-eyed Trump-watchers spotted in Trump Force One when it was flying to New Hampshire, tucked away under his desk while he was being photographed.

———◆———

'I don't do the email thing,' he told a court in July 2015. Social media is his thing and he was ahead of the curve. Nevertheless, he said: 'I have some of the best websites in the world.'

He also said he heard that HealthCare.gov cost $5 billion – which is not true – and joked he builds websites for $3. He must be employing Mexicans.

———◆———

While being a driver in other areas of his life, he told *Golf Magazine* in November 1993: 'I've always been a good chipper and putter. I have great feel. I don't know why. I can feel the putt when I stand over it. I kill guys with my putting.'

Even before *The Apprentice*, he was swamped with TV offers.

'All the networks wanted to do a reality show with me,' he told the *San Francisco Chronicle* in March 2004. 'They wanted to follow me down the hallway with a camera and into meetings. But I am by far the largest developer in the city now, and you can't get any business done that way.'

Trump was asked to host *Saturday Night Live*, which competed in the same time slot as Howard Stern's TV show, where he was a frequent guest. Trump said he would consider the offer but would have to check with Stern first. 'I don't want to mess up Howard's ratings,' he told the *Chicago Tribune*.

There is no doubting his business acumen, though. 'Generally when I become more involved in a company … they tend to work,' he told *Reno Gazette-Journal* in February 2004.

Plainly he was cut out to be president, even as early as 1999 when he told *Saturday Today*: 'This country is essentially in huge debt. And who understands debt better than I?'

———◆———

Of course, it helps to be a genius. He told Wolf Blitzer on CNN's *Late Edition* in 2004: 'All men are not created equal. Some are born with a genius and some are born without. Now, you need that. If you don't have that, you can forget it.'

So Thomas Jefferson was wrong.

———◆———

'Watch, listen, and learn,' were his watchwords according to his book *Trump: The Way to the Top*. 'You can't know it all. No matter how smart you are…'

This is not the impression that he gave during the debates, but then: 'I'm not a debater,' he told ABC News. 'I've never debated before.'

———◆———

'I am the American dream, supersize version,' The Donald admitted modestly in *The America We Deserve*.

———◆———

Asked by ABC news anchor George Stephanopoulos why he was topping the polls, he said: 'I think that people see me as somebody that loves the country. But maybe even more importantly will not let our great country be ripped off by so many others. Everybody is ripping us. And I think they see that. They think I'm a smart guy. They think I have done well in all of that. But maybe above all, they see a person that loves this country, is passionate about this country and will not let China and OPEC and these people take advantage of us any longer. I will tell you, if oil goes up any higher, this country will have a major, major economic collapse. We cannot afford it. We cannot allow it to happen. And I think they see me as a smart, tough guy.'

That was in 2011.

Earlier in that same interview, he said: 'Oil prices might go down. Because there's plenty of oil, all over the world. Ships at sea. They don't know where to dump it. I saw a report yesterday. There's so much oil, all over the world, they don't know where to dump it. And Saudi Arabia says, "Oh, there's too much oil." They came back yesterday. Did you see the report? They want to reduce oil production.'

And he was right. Oil prices went up, then they came down again.

Addressing a rally held on Capitol Hill to protest the Iran nuclear deal, he said: 'We will have so much winning if I get elected that you may get bored with winning. Believe me, I agree, you'll never get bored with winning.'

In The Donald's most recent book, *Crippled America*, he writes: 'I'm a really nice guy, believe me, I pride myself on being a nice guy but I'm also passionate and determined to make our country great again'. Elsewhere in the book, he says he is also:

> 'A really nice guy.'
> 'An unstoppable force.'
> 'Not a politician.'
> 'A practical businessman.'
> 'A very successful businessman.'
> 'A tough and demanding boss.'
> 'A winner.'
> 'Good at reading.'
> 'A businessman with a brand to sell.'
> 'A fighter.'
> 'A realist.'
> 'A competitor.'
> 'A nice guy.'
> 'Proud to be an American.'
> 'Proud and grateful to be an American.'
> 'A Christian.'
> 'A conservative Republican.'
> 'A conservative person.'
> 'Rich.'

6

We Shall Overcomb

' I have a great relationship with the blacks. I've always had a great relationship with the blacks,' he told New York state's Capital District's live radio Talk 1300 in Albany in April 2011. However, his insistence that Barack Obama had been born in Kenya and was thus ineligible to be President brought accusations of racism.

'I don't have a racist bone in my body,' he insisted on *Entertainment Tonight* in July 2015.

However, in his book *Trumped!* former president of Trump Plaza Hotel and Casino John R. O'Donnell claimed that Donald Trump had once said, in reference to a black accountant at Trump Plaza: 'Laziness is a trait in blacks.' He also told O'Donnell: 'Black guys counting my money! I hate it. The only kind of people I want counting my money are short guys that wear yarmulkas every day.'

So Donald's not an anti-Semite, then. He is a great supporter of Israel.

Trump hit back in typically robust style, telling *Playboy* magazine in 1999: 'The stuff O'Donnell wrote about me is probably true. The guy's a f**king loser. A f**king loser. I brought the guy in to work for me; it turns out he didn't know that much about what he was doing. I think I met the guy two or three times total. And this guy goes off and writes a book about me, like he knows me!'

———◆———

Donald pointed out that an African American had once won *The Apprentice* – proof that he is not racist. He told Fox News: 'Well, you know, when it comes to racism and racists, I am the least racist person there is. And I think most people who know me would tell you that. I am the least racist, I've had great relationships. In fact, Randal Pinkett won, as you know, on *The Apprentice* a little while ago, a couple of years ago. And Randal's been outstanding in every way. So I am the least racist person.'

In fact, Donald wished he was black. He told the NBC News special *The R.A.C.E.* in 1989: 'A well-educated black has a tremendous advantage over a well-educated white in terms of the job market. I think sometimes a black may think they don't have an advantage or this and that... I've said on one occasion, even about myself, if I were starting off today, I would love to be a well-educated black, because I believe they do have an actual advantage.'

———◆———

Donald is insistent on the point. In an interview with CNN's Anderson Cooper in July 2005, he said: 'I have a great relationship with African Americans, as you possibly have heard. I just have great respect for them and you know they like me. I like them.'

This interview took place in the wake of the case of Sandra Bland, the Illinois woman stopped while driving in Waller County, Texas for failing to signal a lane change. The police officer got her out of the car, threatened to 'light her up', put her on the ground and handcuffed her. Three days later she was found dead in jail. The medical examiner ruled that it was suicide.

Asked whether he thought this happened to African Americans more often, Trump said: 'I hope it doesn't but it might… The answer is, it possibly does. It shouldn't and it's very sad…'

———◆———

There is one African American man he does not have much time for, however. 'Our great African American President hasn't exactly had a positive impact on the thugs who are so happily and openly destroying Baltimore!' he tweeted on 28 April 2015 after the rioting there following the death in police custody of twenty-five-year-old African American Freddie Gray. President Obama said there was 'no excuse' for violence.

———◆———

On the 'Black Lives Matter' campaign that sprung up after a number of black people died in police custody, Donald

Trump told Fox News: 'I think they're trouble. I think they're looking for trouble. I looked at a couple of people that were interviewed from the group. I saw them with hate coming down the street last week talking about cops and police and what should be done to 'em [and] that was not good. And I think it's a disgrace that they're getting away with it.'

He condemned the Democrats for pandering to the movement.

'I think it's disgraceful the way they're being catered to by the Democrats, and it's going to end up kicking them you know where,' he said.

He also criticized former Secretary of State Colin Powell for speaking out on the issue.

'He's obviously catering to somebody. I don't know who he's catering to,' said Trump. 'I was watching the head of Black Lives Matter being interviewed the other night, and I said to myself, give me a break.'

◆

He feels for the brothers, though. 'Sadly, because President Obama has done such a poor job as president, you won't see another black president for generations!'

◆

He knew who to blame. 'Sadly, the overwhelming amount of violent crime in our major cities is committed by blacks and Hispanics – a tough subject – must be discussed,' he tweeted on 5 June 2013.

Then he got down to the figures: '80% of all the shootings in New York City are blacks. If you add the Hispanics, that figure goes to 98%, 1% white.'

The Huffington Post speculated that the statistics Trump had borrowed originated from a NYPD 2012 New York City enforcement report, which found that of 662 shooting suspects who were racially identified, 78.2 per cent were black, 18.9 per cent were Hispanic and 2.4 per cent were white. Close, but no cigar.

On 22 November 2015, he tweeted: 'Says crime statistics show blacks kill 81 per cent of white homicide victims.' He also tweeted an image purporting to be the USA Crime Statistics for 2015, next to a dark-skinned man with a hand-gun. This showed:

> Blacks killed by whites – 2%
> Blacks killed by police – 1%
> Whites killed by police – 3%
> Whites killed by whites – 16%
> Whites killed by blacks – 81%
> Blacks killed by blacks – 97%

The image cites the 'Crime Statistics Bureau – San Francisco' and the figures purport to be those for 2015; the year was not over and no official figures had been released. However, the FBI's figures for 2014 were:

> Blacks killed by whites – 8%
> Whites killed by whites – 82%
> Whites killed by blacks – 15%
> Blacks killed by blacks – 90%

Some discrepancy here. Several news organizations pointed out that that 'Crime Statistics Bureau' did not exist and no similar body was located in San Francisco. The Pulitzer Prize-winning fact-checking website PolitiFact gave the tweet the rating: 'Pants on Fire'.

'I've been challenged by so many people and I don't frankly have time for total political correctness. And to be honest with you, this country doesn't have time either,' he said in the Grand Old Party's primary debate on 6 August 2015.

But he does know the ropes.

'I can be very politically correct,' he told *CEO Wire* in July 2004. 'I went to the Wharton School of Finance.'

Sadly, he left there in 1968, some years before third-wave feminism came crashing to shore.

He could be politically correct, but he just doesn't want to be. Back in 2000, when Donald Trump was just a business-man, he told *The Advocate*: 'I'm not running for office. I don't have to be politically correct. I don't have to be a nice person. Like I watch some of these weak-kneed politicians, it's disgusting. I don't have to be that way. One of the key problems today is that politics is such a disgrace. It's a media circus freak show. Good people don't go into government.'

But when he did run for office, it made no difference. On the campaign trail in September 2015, he told business leaders in South Carolina: 'I'm so tired of this politically correct crap.'

With that, he ducked out of the media circus and decided that he was too good to go into politics. Or rather...

—◆—

As a red-blooded man, Donald went out specifically to woo the women's vote. 'I cherish women. I want to help women. I'm going to be able to do things for women that no other candidate would be able to do,' he told CNN on 9 August 2015.

'I will be so good to women,' he said the following day.

CBS got: 'I will be phenomenal to the women. I mean, I want to help women.'

While he told ABC: 'I pay them a tremendous amount of money. They make money for me.'

He was a champion of women in the workplace: 'I've hired women, I have thousands working for me right now. They're doing phenomenally well in the top levels.'

—◆—

He offered a job to a woman veteran and a survivor of the 9/11 attacks, after praising the 'smart' yellow two-piece suit she was wearing. When she gave him a hug and kissed him on the cheek, he said: 'Thanks sweetie. That's nice.' This was seen as patronizing, and she would not be one of the all-male panel of five advisers on foreign policy he was currently unveiling.

Women are not the weaker sex, he maintains. 'The smart ones act very feminine and needy, but inside they are real killers.' Was he thinking of Hillary?

'I have seen women manipulate men with just a twitch of their eye – or perhaps another body part.' Perhaps not.

Consequently they do well on reality TV shows: 'It's certainly not groundbreaking news that the early victories by the women on *The Apprentice* were, to a very large extent, dependent on their sex appeal.'

Then there are nagging wives: 'When a man has to endure a woman who is not supportive and complains constantly about his not being home enough or not being attentive enough, he will not be very successful unless he is able to cut the cord.' Don't forget the pre-nup.

'One thing I have learned,' says Donald. 'There is high maintenance. There is low maintenance. I want no maintenance.'

But The Donald has little time for wives (unless they are former lingerie models): 'It's all in the hunt and once you get it, it loses some of its energy. I think competitive, successful men feel that way about women.'

And Melania was not pulling her weight. 'She's not giving me 100 percent,' he told *Time* magazine. 'She's giving me 84 per cent, and 16 per cent is going toward taking care of children.'

He knows his attitude is a vote loser. 'When a man leaves a woman, especially when it was perceived that he has left for a piece of ass – a good one! – there are 50 per cent of the population who will love the woman who was left,' he said after he left Ivana for actress and model Marla Maples. Adding: 'I would never buy Ivana any decent jewels or pictures. Why give her negotiable assets?'

The Donald is puzzled by any negative reaction.

'I don't know why, but I seem to bring out either the best or worst in women,' he said.

While The Donald does not objectify women, he was clearly proud of his beauty pageants, particularly Miss Universe.

'This is a real beauty contest,' he told the *New York Daily News*. 'Others, such as Miss America, are not really beauty contests because they judge a great deal on talent. Miss Universe is all about beauty.'

All that talent got in the way.

'Miss Universe has the best-looking girls in the world,' he said. 'They're much better-looking than the Miss America contestants.'

He rued there was a downside to owning beauty pageant – he had to wait until it was all over before he could date any of the contestants.

'I don't think it would be a conflict of interest if it was after the pageant,' he said. 'Of course, it hasn't happened. Hopefully, it will crop up at some point in the future.'

Beauty pageants and real estate development are much the same thing to Donald.

'Beauty and elegance, whether in a woman, a building, or a work of art is not just superficial or something pretty to see,' he said in *Trump 101: The Way to Success*. Donald would not like anyone to think he was superficial.

'What I do is successful because of the aesthetics,' he told *The New York Times*. 'People love my buildings and my pageants.'

On second thoughts, while promoting Miss USA in the Ozarks in Associated Press: 'Usually, I build buildings. I have to deal with the unions, the Mob, some of the roughest men you've ever seen in your life. I come here and see these incredible beauties. It's a lot of fun.'

And he was not shy about his reasons for owning the show.

'I was a great genius in the eighties,' he said in Branson, Missouri. 'Then I was a great moron in the early nineties. That's probably why I bought this pageant – so I could get a date. Now they call me a genius again. It's great.'

◆

He showed his grasp of aesthetics again when he was interviewed by a female reporter, who asked what he looked for in a future Miss USA.

'Well, obviously it's great outer beauty,' he replied. 'I mean, we could say politically correct that look doesn't matter, but the look obviously matters. Like, you wouldn't have your job if you weren't beautiful.'

He is unashamed.

'Good looks had been my top – and sometimes, to be honest, my only – priority in my man-about-town days,' he said.

◆

He knows this is wrong. In 2001, he told a Women's Chamber of Commerce at his Mar-a-Lago estate in Palm Beach, Florida: 'I love looking at the models. ... Isn't that disgusting? The women here are going to walk out saying, "Isn't that guy a terrible, terrible barbarian?"'

Nevertheless, he founded the modelling company Trump Model Management, which brought fashion models to the US. One of them was Melanija Knavs, who appeared nude on the cover of *GQ* before becoming the third Mrs Trump.

◆

Beauty pageants could get you into trouble, though. When Donald Trump took over Miss Universe, Miss USA and Miss Teen USA in 1996, he began one of his long-running battles with women – or 'telling it like it is', as he would put it.

The Venezuelan beauty Alicia Machado was Miss Universe. Soon after winning the title, she began to put on a few pounds. Donald Trump told Howard Stern that she was 'an eating machine'. At the 1997 Miss Universe Pageant in Miami, although she had gone on a crash diet, Donald complained: 'From my position offstage, I was able to glance up to the green room occasionally. I could just see Alicia Machado, the current Miss Universe, sitting there plumply.'

By then, Donald was carrying a few extra pounds, too.

'God, what problems I had with this woman,' he went on. 'First, she wins. Second, she gains fifty pounds. Third, I urge the committee not to fire her. Fourth, I go to the gym with her, in a show of support. Final act: She trashes me in *The Washington Post* – after I stood by her the entire time. ... Anyway, the best part about the evening was the knowledge that next year, she would no longer be Miss Universe.'

Alicia went on to have a successful career in Spanish-language films. She was the only Miss Universe to pose nude in *Playboy* magazine and her engagement was broken off after she was filmed having sex with another contestant on a reality TV show (not *The Apprentice*). However, she did take after her mentor in making startling tweets.

Concerned by North Korea's artillery attack on a South Korean island in 2010, she got muddled when tweeting for world peace, something all Miss Universes are in favour of: 'Tonight I want to ask you to join me in a prayer for peace, that these attacks between the Chinas do not make our situation worse,' she tweeted on her @aliciamachado77 account.

Her gaffe unleashed a rush of insulting posts, prompting her to go offline. 'I now have a lot of psychopaths on the account and it's best I start another one, kisses,' she signed off.

A would-be commander-in-chief, Donald was clear where he stood on sexual assault in the military.

On 7 May 2013, he tweeted: '26,000 unreported sexual assaults in the military – only 238 convictions. What did these geniuses expect when they put men & women together?'

Following up with: 'The Generals and top military brass never wanted a mixer but were forced to do it by very dumb politicians who wanted to be politically C!'

Donald faced a predictable backlash when he said that, if abortion was banned, 'There has to be some form of punishment.'

'For the woman?' he was asked.

'Yes,' he replied.

Quickly he slammed on the brakes and issued a statement

saying that the doctor or any other person performing the illegal act were the ones who should be punished.

Donald certainly did not say: 'You cannot rape your spouse.' That was his campaign manager Michael Cohen when questioned over a story in Harry Hurt's 1993 book *Lost Tycoon: The Many Lives of Donald J. Trump*, where Ivana allegedly described one sexual encounter with her ex-husband as a 'violent assault', going as far as to characterize it as rape.

At the time of the book's publication, Ivana walked away from the rape accusation, saying: 'I do not want my words to be interpreted in a literal or criminal sense.'

The story, she said, was 'totally without merit.'

Cohen quickly apologized. Trump's lawyers insisted that a statement from Ivana be placed in the front of the book where she described an occasion of 'marital relations' during which 'I felt violated, as the love and tenderness, which he normally exhibited toward me, was absent... During a deposition given by me in connection with my matrimonial case, I stated that my husband had raped me,' the statement read. 'I referred to this as a "rape," but I do not want my words to be interpreted in a literal or criminal sense.'

———◆———

The Donald has no fear of losing the gay vote. He told *Playboy*: 'I know politicians who love women who don't even want to be known for that, because they might lose the gay vote, OK?'

———◆———

BMV

READ MORE SPEND LESS
471 BLOOR STREET WEST
TORONTO
416-967-5757
HST #88221595

04/07/2018   2:32PM   0001
000001#6701

NEW BOOKS	**1**	14 $8.99
NEW BOOKS	**1**	14 $6.99
MDSE ST		$15.98
HST5%		$0.80

***TOTAL $16.78
CASH $50.00
CHANGE $33.22

B-rV

1122 SCREMO STREET
WEST SCREMO 820 8 47U
PHONE# 815-138-3757
815-138-3757

1000 M3:55PM

CASH $20.00
CHANGE $33.00

TOTAL $16.78

Speaking about same-sex marriage, Trump told *The New York Times*, 'It's like in golf. ... A lot of people – I don't want this to sound trivial – but a lot of people are switching to these really long putters, very unattractive. It's weird. You see these great players with these really long putters, because they can't sink three-footers anymore. And I hate it. I am a traditionalist.'

Don't worry. He also said: 'I have so many fabulous friends who happen to be gay, but I am a traditionalist.'

He also has a long putter. Or so he says.

There is a side to Donald Trump that is positively New Age. He is an unlikely convert to feng shui, but has been widely quoted on the subject.

After consulting feng shui master Pun-Yin about the Trump International Hotel & Tower on Columbus Circle, he told *Prestige* magazine: 'It certainly didn't hurt us in any way. Feng shui creates a balance that I believe adds to the comfort zone of rooms and space, and that is felt by guests and residents.'

He gave a politician's argument for using it: 'It's important to adhere to the principles of a large group of people that truly believe these principles, and if they believe them, then that's good enough for me.'

Then there was the more hardheaded approach: 'You don't have to believe in feng shui, I do it because it makes me money.'

7

Hot Air

Donald has clear ideas on global warming and a great many Americans agree with him, except the scientists, of course.

'This very expensive GLOBAL WARMING bullshit has got to stop. Our planet is freezing, record low temps, and our GW scientists are stuck in ice,' he tweeted on 2 January 2014, after Russian research vessel MV *Akademik Shokalskiy* got stuck in the Antarctic pack ice for ten days. When a Chinese icebreaker went to the rescue, it got stuck as well.

In November 2012, he tweeted: 'It's freezing and snowing in New York – we need global warming!' This was in the wake of a storm that may or may not have been caused by climate change. Snowfall in Central Park reached 4.7 inches (120 mm), a daily record. Only ten days earlier, New York had been hit by Hurricane Sandy, flooding streets, tunnels and subway lines, and cutting power around the city.

◆

Curiously, cold weather hits North America every winter.

'It's snowing & freezing in NYC. What the hell ever happened to global warming?' he tweeted on 21 March 2013.

'Ice storm rolls from Texas to Tennessee – I'm in Los Angeles and it's freezing. Global warming is a total, and very expensive, hoax!' he tweeted on 6 December 2013.

'We should be focused on clean and beautiful air – not expensive and business closing GLOBAL WARMING – a total hoax!' he tweeted on 28 December 2013.

'NBC News just called it the great freeze – coldest weather in years. Is our country still spending money on the GLOBAL WARMING HOAX?' he tweeted on 25 January 2014. Toledo suffered its snowiest and the sixth coldest January on record. A 2009 study by MIT found that such events were increasing and may be caused by the rapid melting of the Arctic ice pack.

'Any and all weather events are used by the GLOBAL WARMING HOAXSTERS to justify higher taxes to save our planet! They don't believe it $$$$!' he tweeted on 26 January 2014. And so it goes on.

◆

After all, it's just weather. The Donald told the *Palin Update* radio show: 'I think Obama just said that the biggest threat that we have on the planet today is climate change, and a lot of people are saying, did he really say that? We have people chopping off heads and he's talking about climate change. I call it weather. I call it weather. You know, the weather changes.'

Renewable energy was not the answer. He told Fox News's Neil Cavuto in March 2012: 'Wind is destroying the environment in many, many places. People are going crazy over the horrible, noisy, disgusting windmills and they are horrible and a horrible intrusion, ruining communities, and solar is weak and has not been effective and is very, very expensive.'

Fossil fuels were the answer.

'We are the actual Saudi Arabia of natural gas, and we could really fuel this country with it,' he told Cavuto. 'We have oil under our feet and we don't drill it. We have so much and yet we don't [take] advantage. And so we are beholden to Saudi Arabia and other countries that laugh at us – and they wouldn't be there except for us...

'It is a lot cheaper, it's a lot cleaner, and yet we don't use it because of a lack of leadership. It is hard to believe, but we just don't use our product – we don't drill what is right under our feet.

'If you go to Saudi Arabia, you will see streets paved with gold – there is nothing but money. And they have done it because of us – we have made it possible for them... We ought to drill our own. We would have plenty for ourselves for hundreds of years into the future.'

Fracking was the best option. On 2 May 2012, he tweeted: 'Fracking will lead to American energy independence. With

[the] price of natural gas continuing to drop, we can be at a tremendous advantage.'

Then on 25 September 2013, he tweeted: 'The shale boom is saving our economy… Good for jobs, national security & trade balance. Frack Now & Frack Fast!'

And the Environmental Protection Agency can frack off. '@BarackObama has increased the EPA budget by over 150%. The EPA is an impediment to both growth and jobs. It sends jobs overseas,' he tweeted on 15 November 2011.

Not that Donald was against the environment per se. 'Wind turbines are a scourge to communities and wildlife. They are environmental disasters,' he tweeted on 23 August 2012. Then again on 14 December: 'Windmills are destroying every country they touch – and the energy is unreliable and terrible.' Cynics have linked this to the losing battle he was fighting with the Scottish authorities over an offshore wind project that he said would ruin the views from his golf course.

Fortunately, Donald knew who to blame for climate change. 'The concept of global warming was created by and for the Chinese in order to make US manufacturing non-competitive,' he tweeted on 6 November 2012. Later, in an interview on *Fox & Friends* he said he had been joking, sort of, then flaunted his erudition.

'I think that climate change is just a very, very expensive form of tax. A lot of people are making a lot of money. I know much about climate change,' he said. 'I've received many environmental awards. And I often joke that this is done for the benefit of China – obviously I joke – but this done for the benefit of China. Because China does not do anything to help climate change. They burn everything you can burn. They couldn't care less. Their standards are nothing. But in the meantime, they can undercut us on price.'

———◆———

And The Donald is an expert in the field.

'Nobody knows more about the environment than I do,' he told a Republican Women's Group who'd gathered in the ballroom of the Treasure Island Hotel in June 2011. 'I receive a lot of environmental awards,' he assured the crowd, to murmurs of approval. 'Green technology is important. But what good is green technology here when China is spewing out crap. We gotta drill in Alaska. We gotta drill. There is so much oil.'

———◆———

Then there is: 'Remember, new "environmentally friendly" lightbulbs can cause cancer. Be careful – the idiots who came up with this stuff don't care,' he tweeted on 17 October 2012.

8

Raging Bull

The Donald may not believe in global warming, but he was happy to issue his own global warning. In 2012, The Donald told Fox News: 'Nobody is more into the military than Donald Trump.' True, from the age of thirteen he attended the New York Military Academy (NYMA). First he was going to kick those Somali pirates' asses. He told the political website *Human Events*: 'Give me one good admiral and a few ships, and I will wipe them out so fast. Can you believe that these guys are taking tankers that are a thousand feet long and cost hundreds of millions of dollars, and just taking them with rowboats? It's hard to believe. One good admiral, that's all I want.'

———◆———

'He is not a war hero,' The Donald said of failed presidential candidate Senator John McCain, who spent five and a half years as a prisoner of war after being shot down over Hanoi in the Vietnam war. 'He's a war hero because he was captured. I like people that weren't captured, OK?'

Donald told biographer Michael D'Antonio: 'I always thought I was in the military.' Apparently his five years at the NYMA gave him 'more training militarily than a lot of the guys that go into the military.'

While Donald could not serve in Vietnam, due to student deferments and a medical disqualification, he was not afraid to put himself in harm's way. He admitted sleeping around during the AIDS epidemic in the 1980s.

'I've been so lucky in terms of that whole world,' he told Howard Stern. 'It is a dangerous world out there it's scary, like Vietnam. Sort of like the Vietnam era. It is my personal Vietnam. I feel like a great and very brave soldier.'

Having survived that, The Donald made his first foray into foreign policy. On 2 September 1987, he spent nearly $100,000 on placing advertisements in *The New York Times*, *The Washington Post*, and *The Boston Globe* with the headline THERE'S NOTHING WRONG WITH AMERICA'S FOREIGN DEFENSE POLICY THAT A LITTLE BACKBONE CAN'T CURE.

Asked in 1990 what President Trump's foreign policy would be, he said: 'He would believe very strongly in extreme military strength. He wouldn't trust anyone. He wouldn't trust the Russians; he wouldn't trust our allies; he'd have a huge military arsenal, perfect it, understand it. Part of the problem is that we're defending some of the wealthiest countries in the world for nothing. ... We're being laughed at around the world, defending Japan.'

But Donald knows that it's not that simple. In a more reflective mood, he asked: 'What does it all mean when some wacko over in Syria can end the world with nuclear weapons?'

'We Americans are laughed at around the world for losing a hundred and fifty billion dollars year after year, for defending wealthy nations for nothing, nations that would be wiped off the face of the earth in about fifteen minutes if it weren't for us. Our "allies" are making billions screwing us.' It's nice to have friends, though.

If attacked, he would come up swinging.

'When somebody tries to sucker punch me, when they're after my ass, I push back a hell of a lot harder than I was pushed in the first place. If somebody tries to push me around, he's going to pay a price. Those people don't come back for seconds. I don't like being pushed around or taken advantage of. And that's one of the problems with our country today. This country is being pushed around by everyone.'

———◆———

Donald is prepared to take on China. On the night of the South Carolina primary, he told supporters: 'The greatest abuse of the country, I have ever seen financially. China. What they've done to us is the greatest single theft in the history of the world. They've taken our jobs. They've taken our money. They've taken everything.'

However, Bloomberg reported that the Trump-branded tower in New Jersey was being funded by Chinese investors who paid cash for visas. Once they had got them, they were not too concerned about making a profit.

———◆———

The Donald is not afraid to alienate his investors, though. He warned them in a speech in 2011: 'Listen, you moth-erf*****s, we're going to tax you 25 per cent.' He also told the audience at a Republican debate in March 2016 that trade with the communist country was not free trade but 'stupid trade' and said China 'dumps everything that they have over here.'

'We can't lose $500 billion a year to China,' he said. 'We can't lose a fortune to Japan.'

A trade war was better 'than losing all of this money.' The US 'rebuilt' China, according to The Donald. 'I love China.

I have many Chinese friends. They can't believe they got away with this.'

Returning to the point when he announced he was running, he said: 'Free trade is terrible. Free trade can be wonderful if you have smart people. But we have stupid people.' Except for Donald, obviously.

The idea was that China was bilking the US for hundreds of billions of dollars by manipulating and devaluing its currency.

'The Chinese leaders are not our friends,' he said in 2011. 'I've been criticized for calling them our enemy. But what else do you call the people who are destroying your children's and grandchildren's future? What name would you prefer me to use for the people who are hell-bent on bankrupting our nation, stealing our jobs, who spy on us to steal our technology, who are undermining our currency, and who are ruining our way of life?' These are bad guys.

'We had the president of China here and we gave him a state dinner. When people are screwing you, you don't give them dinner,' he told Republican women in Las Vegas in 2011. 'This year China is going to make from this country, $300 billion. Why shouldn't we make $300 billion?'

It's all about the bottom line.

Again, in July 2015, in South Carolina, he said: 'We give state dinners to the heads of China. I say, "Why are you doing state dinners for them? They're ripping us left and right. Just take them to McDonald's and go back to the negotiating table." It's true!'

◆

That same year he was insistent that he had nothing against the people of China. 'I know the Chinese. I've made a lot of money with the Chinese, I understand the Chinese mind,' he told Xinhua, the official news agency of the People's Republic of China, in April 2011. The same month he told *Time* magazine: 'I did very well with Chinese people. Very well. Believe me.'

This is because, in his busy life, he has taken time to study the Orient. 'I've read hundreds of books about China over the decades,' he told Xinhua. These are twenty of the books he named off the top of his head:

1. *The Party* by Richard McGregor
2. *On China* by Henry Kissinger
3. *Mao: The Untold Story* by Jung Chang
4. *Tide Players* by Jianying Zha
5. *One Billion Customers* by James McGregor
6. *The Coming China Wars* by Peter W. Navarro
7. *The Beijing Consensus* by Stefan Halper
8. *China CEO* by Juan Antonio Fernandez and Laurie Underwood
9. *Poorly Made in China* by Paul Midler

10. *CHINA: Portrait of a People* by Tom Carter
11. *The Man Who Loved China* by Simon Winchester
12. *China Shakes the World* by James Kynge
13. *Mr. China* by Tim Clissold
14. *Country Driving* by Peter Hessler
15. *The Dragon's Gift* by Deborah Brautigam
16. *Factory Girls* by Leslie T. Chang
17. *The Heavenly Man* by Brother Yun
18. *Seven Years in Tibet* by Heinrich Harrer
19. *Battle Hymn of the Tiger Mother* by Amy Chua
20. *1421* by Gavin Menzies

The subtitle of the US edition of *1421*, of course, is *The Year China Discovered America*. Anyone would find that humbling.

But America had recently been rediscovered by China, not in a nice way.

'Our country is in serious trouble,' said Donald. 'We don't have victories any more. We used to have victories, but we don't have them. When was the last time anybody saw us beating, let's say, China in a trade deal? They kill us. I beat China all the time. All the time …

'I just sold an apartment for $15 million to someone from China. Am I supposed to dislike them?' The biggest Chinese bank had its US headquarters in Trump Tower. 'People say you don't like China. No, I love them. … I have many Chinese friends. They live in my buildings all over the place.'

◆

The problem is 'their leaders are much smarter than our leaders. And we can't sustain ourselves with that. It's like, take the New England Patriots and Tom Brady and have them play your high school football team.' Donald has always been a keen sportsman. You can tell from his waistline.

Consequently, he asked: 'Why is Obama playing basketball today? That is why our country is in trouble!'

◆

But Donald never takes his eye off the ball. 'China is upset because of the way Donald Trump is talking about trade with China. They're ripping us off, folks. It is time. I'm so happy they're upset. They haven't been upset with us in thirty years.... I'm not talking about war. But they have waged economic war against us,' he told a rally on Staten Island.

◆

'When did we beat Japan at anything?' asked Donald when announcing he was running for the nomination. 'They send their cars over by the millions, and what do we do? When was the last time you saw a Chevrolet in Tokyo? It doesn't exist, folks. They beat us all the time.' Well, there was the small matter of World War II, and America must take some credit for the post-war resurgence of Japanese industry during the Allied occupation. Even before the war, Japan had taken the US as its model.

No matter how victorious the Japanese are, Donald still comes out on top. When asked how much he was worth in 1989, he told *Time* magazine: 'Who the f**k knows? I mean, really, who knows how much the Japs will pay for Manhattan property these days?'

But he would know how to deal with them. After negotiations with Japan on the Trans-Pacific Partnership, a free-trade deal, were held up by the concerns of Japanese farmers, he said: 'If I was the negotiator for that deal, you'd have so much food pouring into Japan right now they wouldn't know what to do with it.'

He would tell them: 'Fellas, you're gonna take our food and you're gonna love our food.'

Raw hamburger, anyone?

Speaking at a campaign event in Wisconsin in April 2016, Donald Trump said Japan should use nuclear weapons to deter North Korea aggression instead of relying on US military protection. There are 54,000 US troops stationed in Japan and a further 28,500 in South Korea.

'I would rather have them not arm, but I'm not going to continue to lose this tremendous amount of money,' he went on. 'And, frankly, the case could be made that let them protect themselves against North Korea. They'd probably wipe them out pretty quick. If they fight, you know what, that'd be a terrible thing. Terrible… But if they do, they do.'

Japan's pacifist constitution, drawn up during the Allied occupation following World War II, prohibits the use of force to settle international disputes.

Likewise, he told CNN: 'We are better off frankly if South Korea is going to start protecting itself… they have to protect themselves or they have to pay us.'

Indeed, on the topic of giving military aid to foreign countries, he told Republicans in Las Vegas in April 2011: 'I'm interested in protecting none of them unless they pay.' Well, that doesn't really count as aid, then.

The problem was that the allies were just not looking after the US.

'If they're not going to take care of us properly, we cannot afford to police the entire world,' The Donald told CNN. 'I'm prepared to walk, and if they don't take care of us properly… they're gonna have to defend themselves.'

He was eager to suck up to the Germans too. When asked what his first action as president would be, he said: 'I'd throw a tax on every Mercedes-Benz rolling into this country and on all Japanese products, and we'd have wonderful allies again.'

One of The Donald's new buddies looks likely to be Russia. Commenting on the antipathy between Vladimir Putin and Barack Obama, he said of Putin: 'I would probably get along with him very well. And I don't think you'd be having the kind of problems that you're having right now.'

Plainly, he is a fan. On 18 December 2015, he told MSNBC: 'He's running his country and at least he's a leader, unlike what we have in this country.'

Ignoring Russia's record in the Ukraine, Trump said: 'I think our country does plenty of killing also.'

And the Russian people reciprocated. In a YouGov survey of over 20,000 adults in every G20 country, he came out ahead of Hillary Clinton as their choice for the next US president in only one place: in Russia, where he led by twenty-one points. She led by more that twenty-one points in more than fifteen other countries. Unsurprisingly, her lead in Mexico was 54 per cent.

Donald had been against the war in Iraq. He told *Esquire* in 2004: 'Hundreds and hundreds of young people killed... and what about the people coming back with no arms and no legs? Not to mention the other side. All those Iraqi kids who've been blown to pieces. And it turns out that all the reasons for the war were blatantly wrong. All this for nothing!'

Then in 2011, he said: 'We went into Iraq because there were weapons of mass destruction! But there weren't any weapons of mass destruction!

'And people said it was all about oil. And I say, well, that would have been a good reason to go in!'

Even if it cost an arm and a leg.

'I'm not a Bush fan, believe me,' he said. 'He got us into Iraq.'

However, he did have time for the Butcher of Baghdad.

'Whether or not you liked Saddam Hussein, he used to kill terrorists,' he told a Republican breakfast meeting in February 2014.

———◆———

Libya was another matter.

'Our leadership is weak and pathetic – we can't even take over Libya,' he told a Republican Women's Group in the ballroom of the Treasure Island Hotel, Las Vegas in June 2011. 'I say, we go into Libya and we take the oil. People say, Donald, that's a sovereign nation. I say, there's no nation!'

———◆———

And Donald wanted that oil. 'Islamic terrorism is eating large portions of the Middle East. They've become rich. I'm in competition with them,' he said when he announced he was running for president.

And he had a plan: 'I do know what to do and I would know how to bring ISIS to the table or, beyond that, defeat ISIS very quickly. And I'm not gonna tell you what it is tonight,' he said in an interview on Fox News in May 2015, adding that he had a 'foolproof' way of destroying the terrorist group.

Asked why he would not tell, he said: 'I don't want the enemy to know what I'm doing. Unfortunately, I'll probably have to tell at some point, but there is a method of defeating them quickly and effectively and having total victory.'

By July he was prepared to divulge his plan: 'I would bomb the hell out of those oil fields. I wouldn't send many troops because you won't need 'em by the time I'm finished.'

It's easy.

'Take back their wealth. Take back the oil. ... You bomb the hell out of them and then you encircle it, and then you go in. Once you take that oil, they have nothing left. And it's so simple.'

That's kinda his plan with Libya and Iraq. He also wanted to get oil out of Canada, but by completing the Keystone Pipeline rather than bombing.

◆

When it came to Iran, there was another crazy warmonger to deal with. In 2011, he tweeted: 'In order to get elected, @BarackObama will start a war with Iran.'

On YouTube in November 2011, The Donald said: 'Our president will start a war with Iran because he has absolutely no ability to negotiate. He's weak and ineffective, so the only way he figures to get re-elected, and as sure as you're sitting there, is to start a war with Iran.'

———◆———

Instead, Obama sent seventy-two-year-old Secretary of State John Kerry, who has three Purple Hearts. War hero, Donald?

'I will stop Iran from getting nuclear weapons,' said The Donald. 'And we won't be using a man like Secretary Kerry that has absolutely no concept of negotiation, who's making a horrible and laughable deal, who's just being tapped along as they make weapons right now and then goes into a bicycle race at seventy-two years old and falls and breaks his leg. I won't be doing that. And I promise, I will never be in a bicycle race – that I can tell you.'

———◆———

The war did not happen and a deal was made with Iran. So during the GOP primary debate in August 2015, The Donald said: 'We're giving them $150 billion dollars plus. I'll tell you what, if Iran was a stock, you folks should go out and buy it right now because you'll quadruple – this, what's happening in Iran, is a disgrace, and it's going to lead to destruction in large portions of the world.'

The Donald had already sent out his appeal to Iran's leaders to let the Americans they were holding go: 'Fellas – and it is fellas, because they haven't figured out that the women are smarter than the men – you've got to let our prisoners go.'

Then there were those pesky Mexicans.

'The Mexican government forces many bad people into our country. Because they're smart. They're smarter than our leaders,' he told NBC News in July 2015.

Returning to the subject at the GOP debate in August, he said: 'Our leaders are stupid, our politicians are stupid, and the Mexican government is much sharper, much more cunning. So they send all their bad ones over because they don't want to have to pay for them and take care of them.'

Only The Donald can deal with the situation.

'Jeb Bush will not be able to negotiate against Mexico,' he told a Lincoln Day dinner in 2015. 'Jeb Bush with Mexico said, "People, come in, they come in, it's an act of love, OK?"'

But he deleted a retweet that read: 'Jeb Bush has to like the Mexican Illegals because of his wife.'

Jeb Bush met his future wife, Columba Garnica Gallo, on a school trip to Mexico in 1970. When they married in Austin, Texas in 1974, she could not speak English. She became a US citizen in 1979. But then, Donald Trump's first wife, Ivana Zelníčková, was born and brought up in Czechoslovakia, later emigrating to Canada. They married in 1977 and she naturalized in 1988. His second wife, Marla Maples, was American. But his third wife, Melanija Knavs, was born in Yugoslavia. She lived in Italy and France, before moving to New York in 1996. They married in 2005 and she took US citizenship the following year. As we shall see shortly, The Donald is tough on illegal immigrants from Eastern Europe.

———◆———

People were streaming across the border, apparently fleeing the economic powerhouse that is Mexico.

'When do we beat Mexico at the border? They're laughing at us, at our stupidity. And now they are beating us economically. They are not our friend, believe me. But they're killing us economically. The US has become a dumping ground for everybody else's problems,' he told an adoring crowd at Trump Tower.

We may need to build a wall to stop impoverished Americans going there illegally to find work.

The website UPROXX scurrilously put a related story on accompanied by a picture of a grey business suit from the 'Donald J. Trump Signature Collection' whose label said: 'Made in Mexico, 100% Wool'.

———◆———

After winning the Super Tuesday primaries, Donald said: 'You look at countries like Mexico, where they're killing us on the border, absolutely destroying us on the border. They're destroying us in terms of economic development.'

The signs were plain to see. As Donald said on CNN in 2011: 'You land your plane at LaGuardia Airport, you go to LaGuardia Airport, it's like a third-world airport.'

He also dissed Reagan National Airport, JFK, Newark and LAX.

'They're like third-world country airports, falling apart,' he said.

So why do US airports suck? 'They have terrazzo floors inside that are so terrible. … They fix 'em with asphalt.'

———◆———

The problem was that Mexico was keeping all its smartest people at home.

'When Mexico sends its people, they're not sending their best,' he said in his declaration speech. 'They're sending people that have lots of problems, and they're bringing those problems with us. They're bringing drugs. They're bringing crime. They're rapists.'

CNN's Don Lemon took him up on this, but Trump defended himself stoutly.

'Oh well, if you look at the statistics on rape, on crime, on everything coming illegally into this country. They're mind-boggling. If you go to Fusion, you will see a story about 80 per cent of the women coming in … go to Fusion, and pick up the stories on rape, and it's unbelievable when you look at what's going on. All I'm doing is telling the truth.'

Lemon pointed out that the story on Fusion TV, a Hispanic channel, talks about women who had been raped coming into the US, not about rapists coming in. To which Trump replied, 'Somebody's doing the raping, Don. The thing is women being raped, I mean somebody's doing it! Who's doing the raping? Who's doing the raping?'

The Fusion story was actually quoting a 2010 Amnesty International report about women immigrants being raped by criminal gangs, traffickers, fellow immigrants and corrupt officials.

———◆———

Again, The Donald in no way wanted to appear inflammatory.

'I love the Mexican people. I've had a great relationship with Mexico and the Mexican people,' he said. 'I'm not talking about Mexico. I'm talking about illegal immigration, and it has to be stopped. It's killing our country. People are pouring over the borders. We have incredible border patrols. These are incredible people, and they can't do anything.'

And it's not just the Mexicans: 'People are pouring into the United States. I guess some come from Mexico, but they come from all over the world. By the way, they come from the Middle East. We don't even know where they come from.'

American was full up to bursting point.

'We're letting in thousands of people. They don't have documentation, they don't have paperwork, we don't know who they are or where they come from.'

———◆———

The answer, famously, was to build a wall. In an interview with David Brody, the Chief Political Correspondent of CBN News, he said: 'I would build a wall like nobody can build a wall. And nobody comes in illegally any more… Nobody can build a fence like me… I build great buildings all over the world. I would have Mexico pay for it. Believe me. They will pay for it because they have really ripped this country off. They have really taken advantage of us both economically and at the border. They will pay for that fence.'

———◆———

And it would not just be any old 2,000-mile-long wall.

'I will build the best wall, the biggest, the strongest, not penetrable, they won't be crawling over it, like giving it a little jump and they're over the wall, it will cost us trillions…,' he told NH1 News in New Hampshire in April 2015. He had already prepared a tender. There was money to be made.

But, hold on. Had he missed a trick?

'And I'll have Mexico pay for the wall. Because Mexico is screwing us so badly. I will take it from out of just a small fraction of the money they've been screwing us for over the last number of years.'

But nobody south of the border appeared to be counting their pennies. So in August, he repeated the point, telling Fox News: 'Mexico, this is not going to continue, you're going to pay for that wall. And they will, because I say so.'

———◆———

Hold on, Donald. Don't you have to get elected first?

When he announced he was running, he repeated the point: 'I will build a great wall – and nobody builds walls better than me, believe me – and I'll build them very inexpensively. I will build a great, great wall on our southern border, and I will make Mexico pay for that wall. Mark my words.'

And with typical intransigence, former president of Mexico Vicente Fox told Fusion TV: 'I'm not going to pay for that f**king wall. He should pay for it. He's got the money.'

The Donald responded: 'The wall just got ten feet taller.'

However, The Donald was willing to make concessions. During the GOP primary debate on 6 August 2015, he said: 'I don't mind having a big, beautiful door in that wall so people can come in to this country… legally.'

He took full credit for raising the issue. 'If it weren't for me, you wouldn't even be talking about illegal immigration,' he said. 'This was not a subject that was on anybody's mind until I brought it up at my announcement. The fact is, since then, many killings, murders, crime, drugs are pouring across the border, our money going out and the drugs coming in. And I said we need to build a wall, and it has to be built quickly.'

Asked if he thought he might be offending Hispanics, he said: 'Well, they shouldn't feel slighted. And what I said was right. This country is becoming a dumping ground for the entire world. The United States. We owe $19 trillion. We're going to be up to $20 and $22 and $24 is a real magic number. That's really a bad number. That's the point of no return.'

Although the wall might make it hard to get to work, Donald told NBC News in July: 'I'll win the Latino vote because I'll create jobs. I'll create jobs and the Latinos will have jobs they didn't have.' The jobs are building a wall. And they are going to need them, if they are going to pay for it. The estimated cost is anywhere between $2.2 billion and $13 billion. On top of that, deportation of the estimated eleven million illegal immigrants is $114 billion.

'I'm leading in the Hispanic vote, and I'm going to win the Hispanic vote,' he said in his speech at the GOP Lincoln Day dinner at Birch Run, Michigan on 11 August 2015. This was because: 'I love the people of Mexico. I respect the people of Mexico. And I respect Mexico.'

—◆—

Interviewed on Spanish language news programme *Noticiero Telemundo* he said: 'The fact is if I were president, believe me. It wouldn't be the way it is now. And I'll tell you this – I'd end up having a better relation with Mexico than the United States has right now. We would cherish each other. Right now there is tremendous animosity between the

United States and Mexico, despite the fact that Mexico's making all the money. They're making all the money. We're getting killed. So I just finish by saying this. I really like Mexico and I love the people of Mexico. There's nothing else to say. If I were president, the United States would be an amazing place again.'

———◆———

'I am extremely, extremely tough on illegal immigration,' he told Fox News in October 2015. 'I'm extremely tough on people coming into this country.'

However, this didn't stop him employing a small army of illegal immigrants to clear the site for Trump Tower, though he denied doing so knowingly.

In court he said that he only learnt that the two hundred Polish workers in his employ might be in the country illegally 'some time after the demolition work'. However, he admitted using the pseudonym 'John Baron' when dealing with their lawyer who was threatened with a $100-million lawsuit if he did not drop the workers' claim for back pay.

'Lots of people use pen names,' he quipped to a reporter. 'Ernest Hemingway used one.'

Well, yes. It was Ernest Hemingway. Indeed, the case, which dragged on for another decade, reads like a work of fiction and was finally 'resolved on terms agreeable to both sides'. But we will never get to enjoy the final chapter as the agreement was placed under seal.

———◆———

Being from immigrant stock himself has given Donald an understandable empathy on this issue. 'My grandparents didn't come to America all the way from Germany to see it get taken over by immigrants. Not on my watch,' he tweeted in September 2015.

In his first book, *The Art of the Deal*, Donald mistakenly claimed that his grandfather immigrated from Sweden. After being challenged on the point, he reneged: 'I was even thinking in the second edition of putting more emphasis on other places,' he said, 'because I was getting so many letters from Sweden: Would I come over and speak to Parliament? Would I come meet with the president?'

In fact, it transpires that his German-born grandfather made his first fortune running boom-town saloons and brothels in Canada during the Gold Rush. He later returned to Germany and had to leave again after being labelled a draft dodger. No parallels there, then.

Addressing 9/11, he told Fox News: 'I believe that if I were running things … I doubt that those people would have been in the country. So there's a good chance that those people would not have been in our country.'

Then, after the San Bernardino shootings in December 2015, he told a rally in Mount Pleasant, South Carolina: 'Donald J. Trump is calling for a total and complete shutdown of

Muslims entering the United States until our country's representatives can figure out what the hell is going on.'

Again, this was an argument for the Second Amendment: 'If there were guns on the other side pointed at the other direction so the bullets are flying both ways you, wouldn't have had that happen.'

And he knows how to deal with Muslims, telling a crowd in South Carolina on 19 February 2016 a fabricated story of General John Pershing summarily executed dozens of Muslim prisoners in the Philippines during the American occupation.

'He took fifty bullets, and he dipped them in pig's blood,' Trump said. 'And he had his men load his rifles and he lined up the fifty people, and they shot forty-nine of those people. And the fiftieth person he said, "You go back to your people and you tell them what happened." And for twenty-five years there wasn't a problem, OK?'

There is no evidence this ever happened.

The moral of this tale, according to The Donald, was: 'We better start getting tough and we better start getting vigilant, and we better start using our heads or we're not gonna have a country, folks.'

He pledged to bring back waterboarding 'and a hell of lot worse' for suspected terrorists.

'You know they haven't been able to define waterboarding,' he said. 'They don't know if it's torture. If it is, it might be a little too tough, we can't be nice.'

Then again, he asked himself: 'Is it torture or not? It's so borderline,' and decided, 'it's like minimal, minimal, minimal torture.'

Yet again: 'Under the definition of torture, no, it's not. It is enhanced interrogation … It does not meet the generally recognized definition of torture.'

He also called his opponent Senator Ted Cruz, whose father was tortured as a young man in Cuba, a 'pussy' for not sharing his zeal for the practice. He was actually repeating what a woman in the audience had shouted out, then he pretended to reprimand her. 'OK, you're not allowed to say and I never expect to hear that from you again. She said – I never expect to hear that from you again – she said he's a pussy,' Trump explained. 'What kind of people do I have here?'

◆

Asked about oil production in Saudi Arabia, he said: 'I have people. I can send two people into a room. One person comes home with the bacon, the other one doesn't. Same, same thing.' Bacon?

◆

On OPEC, he said: 'We have nobody in Washington that sits back and says, "You're not going to raise the f**king price."'

There's a handful more countries alienated.

Never mind. The Donald is an ace negotiator when it comes to dealing with foreign countries.

'I know the smartest negotiators in the world,' he said in his announcement speech. 'I know the good ones, I know the bad ones, I know the overrated ones. You got a lot of them that are overrated. They're not good, they think they are, they get good stories, 'cause the newspapers get buffaloed. But they're not good. But I know the best negotiators in the world. I'd put them one for each country. Believe me, folks, we'd do very well.'

A safe pair of hands.

Then on 6 May 2016, he recommended that he thought the UK should leave the EU – saying: 'I would say they're better off without it, personally, but I'm not making that as a recommendation, just my feeling' – thereby giving a boost to the remain campaign. Apparently the problem, in The Donald's eyes, is immigrants – Mexicans? No, Muslims.

9

Hung Like A Trumpette

Donald Trump is always eager to flaunt his prowess in every field. So after Republican rival Marco Rubio poked fun at the size of Donald's hands – saying: 'Have you seen his hands? And you know what they say about men with small hands?' – Donald responded: 'He referred to my hands – if they're small, something else must be small. I guarantee you, there's no problem. I guarantee.'

We need to be careful here as artist Illma Gore was threatened with a lawsuit over her nude portrait of Donald Trump with a tiny penis. She says she has received death threats, been threatened with rape and physically attacked by people claiming to be Trump supporters.

The image went viral after she published it on her Facebook page. It was banned from public display in the US, but went on show in the Maddox Gallery in London where it was valued at up to £1 million. Then, on the other hand, there is always the Trump Tower to take into consideration.

For Donald, there had never been the tiniest cause for concern in that area, of course.

'I've never had any trouble in bed,' he wrote in *Surviving at the Top* in 1990. And in 1988, he told the *New York Post*: 'My fingers are long and beautiful, as, it has been well been documented, are various other parts of my body.' He has yet to produce the documentation. At least Obama came up with his birth certificate, eventually. Maybe Donald is waiting until he's in the White House.

Donald did offer to flash his manhood at attorney Gloria Allred in 2012. She was representing Jenna Talackova, a transgendered beauty queen disqualified from competing in Miss Universe Canada, which Trump co-owns, because she was not a 'naturally born' woman.

'[Talackova] did not ask Mr Trump to prove that he is a naturally-born man, or to see the photos of his birth, to view his anatomy, to prove that he was male,' Allred said. 'It made no difference to her. Why should it have made a difference to him?'

Trump called celebrity news website TMZ, offering to show Allred his genitals.

'I think Gloria would be very, very, very impressed with me,' he said. 'I think she'd have a whole, brand-new image of Donald Trump.'

Ms Allred, scarcely believing her luck, declined the offer.

Despite this slight, Donald backed down and Jenna was allowed to compete.

———◆———

The secret was simple. 'I like thinking big,' he tweeted in December 2012. 'If you're going to be thinking anything, you might as well think big.'

———◆———

Donald certainly had no problem dating.

'If I told the real stories of my experiences with women, often seemingly very happily married and important women, this book would be a guaranteed best-seller (which it will be anyway!). I'd love to tell all, using names and places, but I just don't think it's right,' he wrote in *Trump: The Art of the Comeback*. This was because they were both 'married and unmarried women'.

But he admitted he was no Casanova.

'If I'd had affairs with half the starlets and female athletes the newspapers linked me with, I'd have no time to breathe,' was his line in *Trump: Surviving at the Top*. And he told *Time* magazine: 'I don't believe in cheating. But if I look at somebody or somebody looks at me, immediately they do Don Juan stories.'

Indeed, he doffs his cap outrageously to Angelina Jolie, saying on *Larry King Live* in 2006: 'She's been with so many guys she makes me look like a baby.'

Nevertheless, he said in the first half of the 1970s: 'I was especially carefree. I had a comfortable little studio apartment in Third Avenue in the city, and I maintained a lifestyle that was fairly commonplace then... I was out four or five nights a week, usually with a different woman each time, and I was enjoying myself immensely.'

———◆———

Back then, before he had become prematurely orange like Ronald Reagan, the raven-haired lothario was big on the club scene and plainly a devil on the dance floor at the height of discomania.

'One of the first things I did was join Le Club, which at the time was the hottest club in the city and perhaps the most exclusive – like Studio 54 at its height,' he said. 'I met a lot of beautiful young single women, and I went out almost every night. Actually, I never got involved with any of them very seriously.'

However, they proved a disappointment.

'These were beautiful women, but many of them couldn't carry on a normal conversation. Some were vain, some were crazy, some were wild, and many of them were phonies.'

The Donald is known as a conversationalist.

I quickly found out that I couldn't take these girls back to my apartment, because by their standards, what I had was a disaster, and in their world appearances were everything.'

It would be some years before he could take them back to his $10-million fifty-room apartment on the sixty-sixth, sixty-seventh and sixty-eighth floor of Trump Tower. In fact, the building only has fifty-eight floors, but he skipped some floor numbers to give his tenants – and, presumably, himself – a psychic boost and make the building seem bigger than it was.

———◆———

But he did not content himself with bimbos picked up in clubs: 'Oftentimes when I was sleeping with one of the top women in the world I would say to myself, thinking about me as a boy from Queens, "Can you believe what I am getting?"'

It should have come as no surprise. He once said of himself: 'Love him or hate him, Trump is a man who is certain about what he wants and sets out to get it, no holds barred.' A wrestling fan, he hosted WrestleMania events and appeared in 'The Battle of the Billionaires'.

———◆———

In his 1990 book *Trump: Surviving at the Top*, he recalled his relationship with celebrity hotelier, the 'Queen of Mean' Leona Helmsley, who was later jailed for tax evasion after boasting to her housekeeper: 'We don't pay taxes; only little people pay taxes.'

Leona took up the dashing young Donald when he was just starting out in the real estate business, while her husband – though worth $6 billion and owner of the Empire State Building – was already in his mid-sixties.

The Donald could not understand it, as he was not tremendously successful at that time. But Leona always liked having him around. At the 'I'm Just Wild About Harry' parties she gave for her husband, he would always be given a great seat, usually right near her, and 'she went around telling everybody that "this young man will be the next Harry Helmsley," that I was the smartest of the smart, and that there was nobody to compete with me. I was very flattered.'

However, Donald found himself on the wrong end of a jealous outburst when he turned up at one of her parties with 'a young and very attractive fashion model' as his date.

'As soon as Leona saw who was with me, she became incensed. "How dare you bring that tramp to one of my parties?" she screamed, looking the girl directly in the eyes.'

The next day, she called him at his office and said: 'You [expletive] son-of-a-bitch. I watched you politicking the room and all of my guests in order to get your convention center passed.'

There was more.

'She also asked that I not bring to her parties "pretty girls" that would make other women in the room look bad.'

Later he regretted his association with Leona Helmsley.

'The real estate business, especially in New York, is full of bullies,' he said.

———◆———

Women did not stop throwing themselves at him even when he was married. He recalled attending a magnificent dinner being given by 'one of the most admired people in the world.' He was seated next to a 'lady of great social pedigree and wealth … one of the biggest of the big.' Her husband was sitting on the other side of the table.

'All of a sudden I felt her hand on my knee, then on my leg. She started petting me in all different ways.' He shot her a quizzical look, saying later, 'I didn't want to make a scene in a ballroom full of five hundred VIPs.'

She then asked him to dance.

'While we were dancing she became very aggressive, and I said, "Look, we have a problem. Your husband is sitting at the table, and so is my wife."'

But her passion was too intense.

'Donald,' she said. 'I don't care. I just don't care. I have to have you, and I have to have you now.'

He promised to call her, provided she stop her amorous behaviour immediately.

Though he had a ring on his finger, women were falling at his feet.

'The level of aggression was unbelievable,' he said. 'This is not infrequent, it happens all the time.'

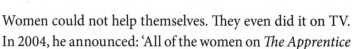

Women could not help themselves. They even did it on TV. In 2004, he announced: 'All of the women on *The Apprentice* flirted with me – consciously or unconsciously. That's to be expected.'

With a string of beautiful wives who see him as the embodiment of the American dream, he is only too well aware of his appeal. 'Part of the beauty of me is that I'm very rich,' he told *Good Morning America* in 2011. Surely Ivana, Marla and Melania would concur.

And in a moment of candour, he said of the man that is Donald Trump: 'Women find his power almost as much of a turn-on as his money.'

On *Celebrity Apprentice* he reciprocated. In another notable demonstration of his commitment to feminism, he told *Playboy* model Brande Roderick: 'Must be a pretty picture, you dropping to your knees.'

But then, when he heard that Mitt Romney, the GOP candidate in 2012, had called on Republicans to stop Trump, he hit back, saying publicly that Romney had begged for his endorsement.

'I could have said, "Mitt, drop to your knees." He would have dropped to his knees,' Trump said, eliciting laughter from the audience.

We are not sure how this turned out. Perhaps Mitt was not in his class. In June 2015, Donald told the *Des Moines Register*: 'I have a Gucci store that's worth more than Romney.'

Some women have slipped through the net, though.

'I only have one regret in the women department,' he said. 'I never had the opportunity to court Lady Diana Spencer.'

In November 1997, three months after Princess Diana had died, NBC's Stone Phillips asked him: 'Do you think you would have seriously had a shot?'

'I think so, yeah,' Trump replied. 'I always have a shot.'

How could she have resisted?

———◆———

He knew where to draw the line, though. In 2003, he told *The Howard Stern Show*: 'I've known Paris Hilton from the time she's twelve. Her parents are friends of mine, and, you know, the first time I saw her, she walked into the room and I said, "Who the hell is that?" ... Well, at twelve, I wasn't interested. I've never been into that. They're sort of always stuck around that twenty-five category.'

After Leona Helmsley, he has plainly gone off hotels.

Later Paris got lucky. As a teenager, she began her modeling career with The Donald's agency Trump Model Management.

———◆———

There were problems closer to home. Asked on ABC's *The View* how he would react if his twenty-four-year-old daughter and former teen model Ivanka posed for *Playboy*, he said: 'It would be really disappointing – not really – but it would depend on what's inside the magazine.' *What's inside the magazine?* It's *Playboy*. Then he added: 'I don't think Ivanka would do that, although she does have a very nice figure. I've said if Ivanka weren't my daughter, perhaps I'd be dating her.'

'Who are you? Woody Allen?' asked *The View*'s co-host Joy Behar.

Later, he told *Rolling Stone* magazine: 'She's really something, and what a beauty, that one. If I weren't happily married and, ya know, her father...'

Plainly the Trumps are a close-knit family.

When Ivanka was just twenty-one Donald was boasting about how hot she was on *The Howard Stern Show*, saying: 'You know who's one of the great beauties of the world, according to everybody? And I helped create her. Ivanka. My daughter, Ivanka. She's six feet tall, she's got the best body. She made a lot money as a model – a tremendous amount.'

The fact that he 'helped create her' surely can't be the reason he told *New York* magazine the following year: 'Every guy in the country wants to go out with my daughter.' They all wanted a strand of his DNA.

Fortunately for all concerned, sex is not his number-one turn-on. In his book *The Art Of The Deal* he said he liked making deals, preferably big deals – 'That's how I get my kicks.'

And on *Saturday Night with Connie Chung*, he raved about the megadeals he was pulling off. 'It's exciting, and part of the reason it's exciting is because they're megadeals, they're important deals, they're glamorous deals,' he said. 'Everybody talks about them, everybody reads about them and writes about them. There's a level of importance there that I think also somewhat turns me on.'

Out on the stump in December 2015, Donald told a meeting in Manchester, New Hampshire once again: 'I respect women, I love women, I cherish women.'

He continued: 'You know, Hillary Clinton said, "He shouldn't cherish". Well, I said, I do cherish, I love women. . . . I will take care of women, and I have great respect for women. I do cherish women. And I will take care of women.'

However, The Donald is also widely quoted saying about women: 'You have to treat them like shit' in *New York* magazine in 1992. How times have changed. In fact, there are some caveats. The article says: 'His contempt for beautiful women who like to be abused is boundless, and he is full of stories of supermodels he might called twelves (not their size), clinging to a rock star's leg and the rock star kicking them away. You have to treat them like s***.'

The article went on to make excuses for him.

'He's seen the disloyalty of wives and widows; a "disloyal lady" like Barbara Walters, who asked him about his divorce on TV when she promised she wouldn't; and major babes who fall for guys with voices and guitars.'

He had dated the nineteen-year-old Italian model Carla Bruni, who reportedly bedded Mick Jagger and Eric Clapton before going on to marry French President Nicolas Sarkozy and become an intimate of Michelle Obama.

'Babes are bad but necessary. "I was getting ready to sack her," he will say weeks later, describes a post-Marla date.

Women are two types for him – those of use, and those he beds, or "sacks," and, of the two, the former probably get more of his heart.'

This was after an incident where he poured wine down the back of Marie Brenner after she wrote a story about his divorce in *Vanity Fair* which he hated.

In a more unguarded moment, talking about the movie *Pulp Fiction* in a TV documentary in 2005, he said: 'My favorite part is when Sam has his gun out in the diner and he tells the guy to tell his girlfriend to shut up. Tell that bitch to be cool. Say: "Bitch be cool." I love those lines.'

One thing that Julie Baumgold certainly got right in her 1992 *New York* magazine piece was that his heart goes out to women who are 'of use' – though his 'sack' at the time was a twenty-five-year-old Victoria's Secret supermodel. He was forty-six at the time and had moved into Trump Tower. And it all came down to dear old ma.

'It's funny,' he said. 'My own mother was a housewife all her life. And yet it's turned out that I've hired a lot of women for top jobs, and they've been among my best people. Often, in fact, they are far more effective than the men around them.'

He is not about to embrace Andrea Dworkin, or even Heidi Cruz, however.

'I'm not a crusader for feminism, and I'm not against it, either. I'm just oblivious to a person's gender when it comes to hiring people and handing out assignments,' he said.

He demonstrated this when he hired Ivana to run the Trump Castle casino in Atlantic City. Then, when he installed Marla Maples, soon to be Mrs Trump Mark II, in a suite in the Trump Regency, Atlantic City, Ivana was promoted, becoming president of the Plaza Hotel in New York.

—◆—

When running for the nomination, Donald made a pledge on equal pay for women, telling a young female questioner: 'You're going to make the same if you do as good a job.' And Trump told Joe Scarborough and Mika Brzezinski of MSNBC's morning show at the time: 'If they do the same job, they should get the same pay.'

That may prove to be a disappointment for some men. At a press conference to announce Ivana's new position as the president of the Plaza hotel, he said: 'I will pay her one dollar a year and all the dresses she can buy!'

Presumably, equal pay in this instance is an incentive for transgendered males. Donald is more politically correct than he realizes. 'I have really given a lot of women great opportunity,' Trump said in one of his more overtly feminist statements.

'Unfortunately, after they are a star, the fun is over for me,' he continued. It is assumed he was talking about his beauty pageants, and maybe that is where he is out of luck. In 1991, he told *The Observer*: 'I'm a bit of a P. T. Barnum. I make stars out of everyone.'

◆

On prenuptial agreements, he said on *This Morning* in January 1998: 'It's a terrible document. It's ugly, it's – it's horrible in almost every way, but you need it. It's very tough to walk up to a woman or a man and say, "Listen, darling, I love you very much, but just in case we get divorced, this is what you're gonna be getting, if it's OK with you."'

They can be useful, though. After his divorce from Ivana, he told *New York* magazine: 'If I didn't have mine, I would not own all these beautiful buildings.'

Ivana unsuccessfully challenged their prenuptial agreement that limited any divorce settlement to $25 million on the grounds that she had contributed to his business by revamping the Plaza. Under the final deal, Trump agreed to pay her $14 million in cash, $350,000 in annual alimony and $300,000 per year for the support of their three children. Ivana also got their mansion in Greenwich, Connecticut and an apartment in Trump Plaza.

◆

Donald explained what had gone wrong: 'My big mistake with Ivana was taking her out of the role of wife and allowing her to run one of my casinos in Atlantic City, then the Plaza Hotel. ... Ivana worked very hard, and I appreciated the effort, but I soon began to realize that I was married to a businessperson rather than a wife.'

Clearly it is not a good idea to let business come between you. But this was not a lesson that Donald had taken to heart by the time of his next outing, with Marla Maples.

'I was bored when she was walking down the aisle. I kept thinking, "What the hell am I doing here?" I was so deep into my business stuff. I couldn't think of anything else.'

———◆———

It was probably a mistake to have the ceremony in the Plaza, then. Perhaps he thought he was marrying the hotel.

'I'm married to my business,' he told *New York* magazine. 'It's been a marriage of love. So, for a woman, frankly, it's not easy in terms of relationships. But there are a lot of assets.'

The New York Times reported: 'The bride is taking her husband's name. The bridegroom is keeping his name, The Donald, a legacy from his former wife, Ivana.'

Writer Julie Baumgold remarked: 'There wasn't a wet eye in the place.'

Others compared it to the wedding of Charles and Diana.

Howard said: 'I give it four months.'

His new wife proved unreasonable.

'Marla was always wanting me to spend more time with her,' he complained. '"Why can't you be home at 5 o'clock like other husbands?" she would ask. Sometimes, when I was in the wrong mood, I would give a very materialistic answer. "Look, I like working. You don't mind traveling around in beautiful helicopters and airplanes, and you don't mind living at the top of Trump Tower, or at Mar-a-Lago, or traveling to the best hotels, or shopping in the best stores and never having to worry about money, do you?"'

There was nothing for it. After three and a half years they split. 'Marla was becoming too obsessive. She's a good girl, but it was becoming too much,' he told the *New York Post*.

Rich and powerful women, such as Kim Basinger, were clamouring at the door of the Trump Tower to see him, he told *People* magazine.

'Competitively, it's tough. It was for Marla and it will be for Carla,' he said.

Nevertheless, he told Associated Press. 'It's one of the worst times in the history of the world to be dating.'

He asked women to have an AIDS test at his doctor's office before he would date them. Meanwhile, Marla was held her to her contract to host the 1997 Miss Universe Pageant and Miss USA Pageant.

———◆———

Hope springs eternal. After two failed marriages, he told Chris Matthews on MSNBC's *Hardball*: 'I believe in the institution of marriage. There's nothing better. It beats being the world's greatest playboy by a million, but sometimes you don't have a choice.'

———◆———

But there's a problem here: 'I love beautiful women, and beautiful women love me. It has to be both ways.'

10

Fat Pigs, Dogs, Slobs and Disgusting Animals

The Donald had a long-running run-in with talk-show host Rosie O'Donnell, who came out as a lesbian in 2002. The row began when she called Trump a 'snake-oil salesman' after he refused to sack Miss USA 2006, Tara Conner, who was accused of excessive drinking, cocaine abuse, and kissing Miss Teen USA Katie Blair in public.

'I wouldn't say I'm an alcoholic,' she told reporters.

'I don't think she denies she's an alcoholic,' said Trump, rallying to her defence.

The next day on *The View*, O'Donnell criticized his decision, saying that Trump was 'not a self-made man' but a 'snake-oil salesman on *Little House On The Prairie*,' and she proceeded to slam his multiple marriages – though she had attended his wedding at the Plaza to Marla Maples – saying he: 'left the first wife, had an affair, had kids both times, but he's the moral compass for twenty-year-olds in America. Donald, sit and spin, my friend.'

Adding insult to injury, O'Donnell pulled her hair across her head in imitation of his famous combover. Then she pointed out that he had gone bankrupt several times – something he vigorously denied, saying that his companies had gone bankrupt, while he himself had remained solvent.

◆

The Donald fired back in *People* magazine: 'You can't make false statements. Rosie will rue the words she said. I'll most likely sue her for making those false statements – and it'll be fun. Rosie's a loser. A real loser. I look forward to taking lots of money from my nice fat little Rosie.'

On CNN's *Anderson Cooper* show, he was more explicit, saying: "Probably I'll sue her. Because it would be fun. I'd like to take some money out of her fat ass pockets.'

He explained that Rosie did not like his beauty pageants and went on: 'If you looked like Rosie you'd be critical of beauty pageants, believe me. Rosie is a very unattractive woman, both inside and out. And as hard as it is to believe, inside is probably uglier than outside, and that's really saying something... But you have to understand, I know Rosie. Rosie's a loser. Rosie's been pulling the wool over people's eyes for a long time. She is a stone cold loser. What she is is a bully. Rosie says a lot of negative things about a lot of people. Nobody... they don't do anything about it. I did something about it.'

◆

Then on *Entertainment Tonight* he laid the venom on with a trowel, saying: 'Rosie O'Donnell is disgusting – both inside and out. If you take a look at her, she's a slob. She talks like a truck driver. How does she even get on television? … Rosie attacked me personally because I was very happy when her talk show failed … Another thing that failed, and this was a real monster, everybody was suing her, was her magazine. Her magazine called *Rosie* was a total disaster. So I love it, I gloat over it, I think it's wonderful, because I like to see bad people fail....'

Worst of all: 'She doesn't have her facts, she'll say anything that comes to mind,' said the notoriously unscripted Donald. 'I mean she's basically a disaster.'

———◆———

And he took personal offence.

'She called me a snake-oil salesman, and, you know, coming from Rosie, that's pretty low, because when you look at her, and when you see the mind, the mind is – is weak. I don't see it. I don't get it. I never understood. How does she even get on television?'

Then he went into *Apprentice* mode.

'If I were running *The View*, I'd fire Rosie. I'd look her right in that fat, ugly face of hers and say, "Rosie, you're fired." We're all a little chubby but Rosie's just worse than most of us. But it's not the chubbiness – Rosie is a very unattractive person, both inside and out. Rosie's a person that's very lucky to have her girlfriend and better be careful or I'll send one of my friends over to pick up her girlfriend. Why would she stay with Rosie if she had another choice?'

Rosie's robust response was to post on her blog: 'i will let u know if the Donald sues me or if Kelli leaves me for one of his pals dont u find him charming.'

---◆---

But Donald was clairvoyant. He told the *New York Post*: 'I think she's a terrible person. I can look at people and see what they are.' That's why you were friends for so many years.

Then he had a go at her now ex-wife. On Fox News he speculated on how Kelli might have explained the couple's relationship to her parents.

'Can you imagine the parents of Kelli … when she said, "Mom, Dad, I just fell in love with a big, fat pig named Rosie?"' he said.

Fortunately, Kentucky Fried Chicken stepped in, in the peace-keeping role. As Tara Conner was from the state of Kentucky, KFC offered a ten-piece meal for Rosie and Donald to share. This was their 'Ten Peace Offering'. A statement from the president and chief concept officer of the KFC Corporation asked: 'Why point fingers when you can lick 'em?'

One can only hope that Colonel Sanders will be step in again in the event of an international crisis.

---◆---

Hostilities resumed in December 2011 when Rosie announced her own forthcoming nuptials with then-girlfriend Michelle Rounds. Donald tweeted: 'I feel sorry for Rosie's new partner in love whose parents are devastated at the thought of their daughter being with @Rosie – a true loser.'

O'Donnell responded: '@realDonaldTrump – wow u r an ass in every way.'

He then trashed her new show on Oprah Winfrey's network, saying it was 'a complete and total disaster'. He also linked it to the falling ratings of Lawrence O'Donnell's MSNBC show, simply because they had the same last name. However, he mistakenly tweeted: 'I hear that dopey political pundit Lawrence O'Donnell, one of the dummer [sic] people on television is about to lose his show – no ratings? Too bad.'

This was rapidly retweeted as: 'I hear that dopey political pundit Lawrence O'Donnell, one of the dumber people on television is about to lose his show – no ratings? Too bad.'

He also paraded his TV-smarts, saying: 'It's really amazing. When I don't like somebody their shows do really badly.'

The Rosie Show was cancelled after five months, but *The Last Word with Lawrence O'Donnell* is still on air, while The Donald is not.

◆

The following year Donald turned his guns on Cher for slamming 2012 Republican candidate Mitt Romney, but took a swing at Rosie in passing by tweeting: '@Cher attacked @MittRomney. She is an average talent who is out of touch with reality. Like @Rosie O'Donnell, a total loser!'

Three months later, there was a shock truce when Rosie had a heart attack and Donald tweeted: '@Rosie, get better fast. I'm starting to miss you!'

Taken by surprise, Rosie tweeted back: 'well thank u donald – i must admit ur post was a bit of a shock … r u trying to kill me?'

———◆———

Cher got another kicking on Fox News, 15 May 2012, when The Donald said: 'Cher is an average talent who's out of touch with reality. Cher is somewhat of a loser. She's lonely. She's unhappy. She's very miserable.'

Cher had been a successful pop act since 1965 with eighty-four charted Billboard Hot 100 singles and forty-five albums – selling 200 million records worldwide – thirteen movies and seven world tours. Lonely, unhappy and miserable? Perhaps.

On November 12, she tweeted: 'I'll NEVER GO TO MACY'S AGAIN! I didn't know they sold Donald Trump's Line! If they don't care that they sell products from a LOUDMOUTH.'

She got the caps-lock key stuck when she added: 'RACIST CRETIN, WHO'D LIE LIKE "HIS RUG" TO GET SOME CHEAP PRESS! I CANT BELIEVE MACY'S THINKS HE'S THE RIGHT "MAN" 2 REPRESENT THEIR NAME!'

Donald returned fire with: '@cher should spend more time focusing on her family and dying career!' The following year she released *Closer to the Truth*, her twenty-fifth studio album. It went to number three, her highest position in the Billboard chart to date.

And he was not going to take that reference to his hair lying down, tweeting: '@cher – I don't wear a "rug" – it's mine. And I promise not to talk about your massive plastic surgeries that didn't work.' Ouch.

In March 2014, he boasted at the Washington Press Club he had vanquished celebrity foes through Twitter, citing Rosie O'Donnell and Cher. Referring to Cher, he said: 'I hit her so hard she still doesn't know what happened… It's the last I heard of her.'

Trump then had 2.6 million followers, or as he put it, 'many, many millions'. True, Cher used an alias when working with the Wu-Tang Clan in 2014, but she posed for fashion designer Marc Jacobs' advertising campaign the following year – hardly out of the limelight.

The battle with Rosie O'Donnell resumed again in April 2014, when Rosie announced that she was undergoing weight-loss surgery, after trashing former co-host of *The View* Star Jones for doing the same thing. Donald pitched in with a tweet that said: 'Rosie O'Donnell just said she felt "shame" at being fat – not politically correct! She killed Star Jones for weight-loss surgery, just had it!'

Rosie's response was terse: 'Donald – go away.'

But he didn't, first welcoming Rosie's return to *The View*, then tweeting: 'Rosie is back on the View which tells you how desperate they must be. It is the standard short term fix and long term disaster.'

An hour later, he followed up with: 'Rosie is crude, rude, obnoxious and dumb – other than that I like her very much!'

Two months later, Rosie blamed Donald for her weight problems in *People* magazine. With typical aplomb, Donald responded by tweeting: 'Rosie – No offense, and good luck on the new show, but remember, you started it!'

◆

In the end, it was Donald who got fired, not Rosie. The network fired him from *The Apprentice* and dropped Miss USA and Miss Universe.

'Due to the recent derogatory statements by Donald Trump regarding immigrants, NBCUniversal is ending its business relationship with Mr. Trump,' a statement from the broadcaster said.

That is not the way Donald tells it.

'They didn't cut ties with me, I cut ties with them,' he said. He gave up hundreds of millions of dollars to run for president. 'They would love me not to be doing this, I will tell you right now… I mean, the top people come to my office and they said, "Please do this."'

◆

Rose O'Donnell left *The View* in February 2015, having split with her wife Michelle.

'Rosie has teens and an infant at home that need her attention,' said Rosie's rep Cindi Berger. 'This has been a very stressful situation. She is putting her personal health and family first. ABC has been wonderfully understanding and supportive of her personal decision to leave.'

Rosie herself explained in a video for her fans: 'The truth is, I had a heart attack two years ago and stress is very bad for a heart-attack survivor. I'm minimizing my stress by leaving *The View*. The stress I'm having at home is not easily as remediable ... There's lots of stuff going on at home.'

Asked about the struggling show, Trump said, 'Well, it's very sad what's happened to *The View* and I predicted that with Rosie O'Donnell it would fail. I guess the prediction is correct, but, I mean she's a total train wreck, so let's see what happens and I hope it works out well. ... I like the show a lot, but let's face it, Rosie is a loser.'

If he can see off Rosie O'Donnell, surely he can take on Vladimir Putin and Kim Jong-un.

———◆———

But Cher was not done yet. She re-entered the fray with another unprovoked attack on his hair.

'Donald Trump can't come up with a hairstyle that looks human, how can he come up with a plan to defeat ISIS,' she retweeted on 16 June 2015.

She continued venting her spleen, saying: 'Donald Trump's ego is so inflated, he might be the Hindenburg! In the dictionary next to "obnoxious asshole".' She even compared him to Hitler.

Donald's only answer was: 'It's amazing how celebrities such as @Cher can say horrible untrue things about Republican politicians and it's considered okay – but you are not allowed to say the truth about @BarackObama.'

That's why The Donald has always said such nice things about Barack Obama.

Fox News's Megyn Kelly reignited the feud, albeit unintentionally, at a Republican debate in August 2015, where she grilled Trump about the derogatory words he'd used to describe women.

'You've called women you don't like fat pigs, dogs, slobs, and disgusting animals,' she began.

'Only Rosie O'Donnell,' Trump interjected.

Which prompted Rosie to tweet: 'try explaining that 2 ur kids.'

The Donald is plainly a man so brimful of testosterone that he is naturally sensitive to hormone levels in others. After his brush with Megyn Kelly, he said: 'You could see there was blood coming out of her eyes. Blood coming out of her wherever.'

He later denied that this was a reference to her menstrual cycle, telling NBC's Chuck Todd on *Meet the Press,* 'Only a deviant would think that'. Plainly, he had given up on the deviant vote.

Donald's campaign manager complained that Kelly was 'totally obsessed with Mr Trump.' Oh God, not another attractive woman falling for The Donald. Does he have to beat them off with a stick?

Donald himself boycotted the next GOP debate that Kelly was moderating, calling Megyn 'a bimbo' and posting seductive photographs of her from a 2010 *GQ* magazine shoot on his official Twitter page.

All of which prompt Cher to tweet: 'Trump NOT Doing FOX Debate Cause Of Megyn Kelly. Some1 Get Him TOE SHOES, fkng PRIMA DONNA. HOW CAN HE FACE ISIS, HE CANT FACE A CHICK ON TV.'

The winner turned out to be Megyn Kelly, when Donald agreed to do a face-to-face interview with her in April 2016.

◆

There were other women in the frame. He called Arianna Huffington, editor-in-chief of *The Huffington Post*, 'a dog', tweeting: '@arianahuff looks? Because she is a dog who wrongfully comments on me.'

And after her husband came out and they divorced, he tweeted: '@ariannahuff is unattractive both inside and out. I fully understand why her former husband left her for a man – he made a good decision.'

Was he expecting to get good press? Does he care?

'Some of the press is scum,' he told a Republican Women's

Group in the ballroom of the Treasure Island Hotel in June 2011.

And when Gail Collins referred to him as a 'financially embattled thousandaire' in a piece called 'Donald Trump Gets Weirder' that April, *The New York Times* columnist said she was sent a copy of the article with her picture circled and 'The Face of a Dog!' written over it.

After *Us Weekly* printed compromising pictures of actor Robert Pattinson's girlfriend Kristen Stewart with director Rupert Sanders, The Donald assumed the agony-aunt role, tweeting: 'Robert Pattinson should not take back Kristen Stewart. She cheated on him like a dog and will do it again – just watch. He can do much better!'

Fact-checkers PolitiFact said while they could not find documentation of an exact time The Donald said 'disgusting animal', he has certainly used both words.

He outraged lawyer Elizabeth Beck in July 2015, calling her 'disgusting' when she asked for a break to pump breast milk for her three-month-old daughter during a hearing he was attending. She told CNN: 'He got up, his face got red, he shook his finger at me and he screamed, "You're disgusting, you're disgusting," and he ran out of there.'

Later he tweeted: 'Lawyer Elizabeth Beck did a terrible

job against me, she lost (I even got legal fees). I loved beating her, she was easy.'

USA Today's fact-check found incidences of The Donald calling Rosie O'Donnell a 'disgusting pig' and 'an animal'. Again, they could not find any instance of him calling any woman a 'disgusting animal'. Oh, that's all right, then.

◆

In 2012, Donald Trump and Bette Midler engaged in a Twitter war, which she started by tweeting: 'The man who has ruined New York seeks to ruin the nation. Show some respect, if not for the man, then for the office.'

Then Bette could not resist going for the hair, tweeting: '60 Shades of Stupidity: Ten extra points for the terrible dye job someone talked him into.'

In an effort to keep his hair on, Donald tweeted back: 'Now grotesque @BetteMidler is into the Trump act – trying to become relevant again.'

Then over the next few minutes came a torrent.

'I never liked @BetteMidler's persona or singing and haven't heard her name in years.'

'But whenever she sees me, she kisses my ass. She's disgusting.'

'@BetteMidler talks about my hair but I'm not allowed to talk about her ugly face or body – so I won't. Is this a double standard?'

He finished off with: 'While @BetteMidler is an extremely unattractive woman, I refuse to say that because I always insist on being politically correct.'

A little too late to be PC now, Donald.

———◆———

When *Sex and the City* star Sarah Jessica Parker was voted the 'Unsexiest Woman Alive' in a 2007 poll for *Maxim* magazine, Donald rather ungallantly tweeted: 'Sarah Jessica Parker voted "unsexiest woman alive" – I agree. She said "it's beneath me to comment on the Obama charitable gift." What's really beneath her?'

The charitable gift was Donald's kind offer to donate $5 million to charity if President Obama released his college records and passport application. Sarah said this was 'offensive and self-serving'.

———◆———

Donald also had a pop at Angelina Jolie on *Larry King Live*, saying: 'Angelina Jolie is sort of amazing because everyone thinks she's like this great beauty. And I'm not saying she's an unattractive woman, but she's not a beauty, by any stretch of the imagination. I really understand beauty. And I tell you she's not.'

And The Donald thinks he knows what he's talking about.

'I do own Miss USA,' he insisted. 'I mean I own a lot of different things. I do understand beauty, and she's not.'

———◆———

Carly Fiorina was the only woman who sought the Republican nomination, so she was bound to come in for some stick because she did not live up to Trump's standards of pulchritude.

He dismissed her challenge on TV, saying: 'Look at that face! Would anyone vote for that? Can you imagine that, the face of our next president?'

He was on solid ground here.

'It's very hard for them to attack me on looks, because I'm so good-looking,' he told NBC's *Meet the Press* in August 2015.

◆

After *The Apprentice* premiered in 2004, Donald went on *The Tonight Show* with the cast of *The View*. Jay Leno got The Donald talking about the great success of *The Apprentice*.

'Star Jones raved about it, as did the others – except for Joy Behar, a woman with no talent and a terrible accent, who again attacked my hair. I've always said that the show would do better without her. I did her a favour by going on the show, and it was not appreciated. Being nice to some people never pays off.'

◆

Of course, Hillary Clinton was his biggest target.

'Hillary Clinton was the worst Secretary of State in the history of the United States,' he said in an interview with NBC News's Katy Tur. 'There's never been a Secretary of

State so bad as Hillary. The world blew up around us. We lost everything, including all relationships. There wasn't one good thing that came out of that administration or her being Secretary of State.'

Hillary naturally responded with a crack about his hairstyle.

'Donald Trump,' she said. 'Finally a candidate whose hair gets more attention than mine.'

However, he did not say: 'If Hillary Clinton can't satisfy her husband, what makes her think she can satisfy America?' The tweet was originated by Texas-cowgirl college student Sawyer Burmeister.

'Sry [sorry] to those offended by me merely making a political joke,' she had tweeted in a follow-up. 'Get some rest, there are more important things in the world to be worried about.'

But by then, the jibe had been retweeted with Trump's Twitter handle.

The *New York Daily News* reported that it had not been retweeted by Trump himself, but by one of the ten staff members who had his social media.

'As soon as Mr Trump saw the tweet, he deleted it,' said one of them, thereby ensuring greater coverage.

There were some women Donald admired, though. He told

ABC News Sarah Palin was 'an amazing woman. You know, she gets knocked by so many people and she just keeps getting back up and up.'

Asked at a town hall meeting in Livingston, New Jersey, whether he would consider Palin as a running mate, he said: 'Sure, I'd choose someone like Sarah Palin. There aren't many people who have as large a base as she's got. Judging from your reactions today – why not? In fact, I'd choose Sarah Palin.'

She may have a big base, but, he also said, 'I would pick somebody that would be a terrific – you know, you have to view it as really who would be a good president in case something happened. But I would – there are many, many people out there that I think would be very good.'

Not Sarah, then.

On more than one occasion he said that he would love to have Oprah Winfrey as his running mate. 'I think Oprah would be great. I'd love to have Oprah – I think we would win easily,' he told ABC News's George Stephanopoulos. He had previously mentioned her as a candidate for vice president in 1999, when he considered running for president of the Reform Party.

To prove that he was not sexist, he bigged-up fellow tycoon and TV personality Martha Stewart.

'Martha's a friend of mine,' he told *Capital Report* on 29 January 2004, 'so I have a little bit of a prejudice in that sense. I know her. She's a good woman. She gets terrible press; she gets an unfair press. She's certainly a tough woman. You know, if Martha were a man, they'd say, "Oh, what a great businessperson. What a tough person," and they'd say it glowingly. But as a woman, there's a double standard. They say she's a – you know, they use the B-word. And the fact is, it's not true. She's a very fine woman. I've known her for a long time, and I think she'll be fine.'

In March 2004, Stewart was convicted of four counts of obstructing justice and lying to Federal investigators over a well-timed stock sale and sentenced to five months in jail.

11

The Art of the Insult

In 1987, Donald Trump published his first book, *Trump: The Art of the Deal*. There is little doubt that he was already very good at it. Since then he has been perfecting the art of the insult. The worst insult in the Trump canon is 'loser'.

Republican political advisor and chief of staff to George W. Bush Karl Rove was a 'total loser'. Republican 'public opinion guru' Frank Luntz was a 'total loser'. British comedian Russell Brand is a 'major loser'!

◆

Then there is 'moron'. Pulitzer-prize-winning journalist George Will was a 'moron'. The moderator of MSNBC's *Meet the Press* Chuck Todd is a 'moron'. Former Secretary of Defense Chuck Hagel was an 'obvious moron'.

◆

That was followed by 'dummy'. Conservative blogger Michelle Malkin was a 'dummy'. NBC *Nightly News* managing editor and anchor Brian Williams was a 'dummy'. Long-serving editor of *Vanity Fair* and co-founder of *Spy* magazine Graydon Carter was a 'dummy'.

◆

Then there were the other Republican contenders for the presidential nomination. 'Truly weird Senator Rand Paul of Kentucky reminds me of a spoiled brat without a properly functioning brain,' The Donald tweeted.

'What a stiff, what a stiff, Lindsey Graham,' he said at an appearance in Bluffton, South Carolina on 21 July 2015. 'A total lightweight. In the private sector, he couldn't get a job. Believe me. Couldn't get a job. He couldn't do what you people did. You're retired as hell and rich. He wouldn't be rich; he'd be poor.'

Earlier in the day, Graham had called Trump a 'jackass'. In response, Trump called Graham an 'idiot' and held up a card that included Graham's personal phone number, then asked his supporters to call Graham. 'I don't know, give it a shot,' he said.

At the same meeting, he said Rick Perry 'put on glasses so people think he's smart.... People can see through the glasses.'

He also said Perry should have an IQ test before they got to the debate stage: 'I think Rick Perry is probably smarter than Lindsey Graham. But what do I know?'

'I'm not a fan of Jeb Bush,' he went on. 'The last thing we need is another Bush.'

George W. Bush, he added, is 'no Einstein', and the only thing the Bush family were good at was 'sitting on boards and picking up checks'.

Rick Santorum? 'I have a big plane. He doesn't.'

'Lyin' Ted Cruz just used a picture of Melania from a shoot in his ad. Be careful, Lyin' Ted, or I will spill the beans on your wife!' The Donald tweeted on 23 March 2016, just before the polls closed for the primaries in Arizona.

In August 2015, he tweeted: 'I just realized that if you listen to Carly Fiorina for more than ten minutes straight, you develop a massive headache. She has zero chance!'

He dismissed the others wholesale for the way announced their candidacy, compared to his discreet launch in the lobby of Trump Tower.

'The other candidates – they went in, they didn't know the air conditioning didn't work. They sweated like dogs. They didn't know the room was too big because they didn't have anybody there. How are they gonna beat ISIS? I don't think it's gonna happen.'

He conceded that they were nice people, but 'people are tired of these nice people', while saying of himself: 'I think I'm a nice person. People that know me, like me.'

We'll have to take that on trust.

And the Democrat hopefuls did not even get a look-in. 'Sorry, there is no STAR on the stage tonight!' he tweeted during their TV debate in October 2015, before writing them off individually. It seems he was auditioning to take over from Simon Cowell on *America's Got Talent*.

◆

Ted Cruz got it in the neck again on the afternoon of the crucial Indiana primary.

'His father was with Lee Harvey Oswald prior to Oswald's being – you know, shot. I mean, the whole thing is ridiculous,' said Donald, linking his last credible rival to the assassination of President John F. Kennedy. 'What is this, right prior to his being shot, and nobody even brings it up? They don't even talk about that. That was reported and nobody talks about it. I mean, what was he doing – what was he doing with Lee Harvey Oswald shortly before the death? Before the shooting? It's horrible.'

The claim came from an unimpeachable source – the *National Enquirer*.

Cruz responded that Trump was a 'narcissist' and a 'pathological liar… straight out of a psychology text book,' and withdrew from the race.

◆

'It's amazing how people can talk about me but I'm not allowed to talk about them,' rues Donald.

He is always being traduced: 'How come every time I show anger, disgust or impatience, enemies say I had a tantrum or meltdown – stupid or dishonest people?'

———◆———

The Speaker of the House of Representatives John Boehner, once tipped for higher office, was known for bursting into tears in public.

'I don't like the crying,' The Donald said. 'I do not like it. I don't understand it. I really like him as a person. I think the crying is an emotional thing that frankly, probably makes him a very nice man. But you know, I don't like to see it in a leader.'

Luckily, Boehner turned on Ted Cruz, calling him 'Lucifer in the flesh'.

———◆———

Of the Republican Governor of Texas Greg Abbott who assumed office in January 2015, Trump said: 'The new governor, Governor Abbott … I see him, he's so vicious. He used to be a really nice guy. He used to come see me for contributions, for support. All of a sudden he wants to show he's a tough guy with Trump. So tough.'

———◆———

He also had words to say about Hillary's rival, the Democratic hopeful Bernie Sanders, whose speech was hijacked by Black Lives Matter protesters in Seattle.

'I would never give up my microphone! I thought that was disgusting. That showed such weakness, the way he was taken away by two young women. The microphone!'

But then Donald's voice is so loud, does he need really a microphone?

◆

'Do you mind if I sit back a little? Because your breath is very bad – it really is,' he told Larry King on national TV.

◆

Many Americans found it insulting that The Donald questioned Barack Obama's eligibility to be president, claiming that he was not a 'natural born citizen of the United States' as required by Section 1 of Article Two of the Constitution.

'His grandmother in Kenya said he was born in Kenya, and she was there and witnessed the birth,' he said on NBC's *Today* show in April 2011.

He then said that he had sent private investigators to Hawaii to examine his birth certificate.

'I have people that have been studying it and they cannot believe what they're finding,' he said. 'I would like to have him show his birth certificate, and can I be honest with you, I hope he can. Because if he can't, if he can't, if he wasn't born in this country, which is a real possibility... then he has pulled one of the great cons in the history of politics.'

◆

At first, he hadn't believed the rumours that Obama had not been born in the US.

'His mother was a hippy. His father was a guy from Kenya who split. There couldn't have been a sophisticated – what is he, Baby Jesus? – there was a sophisticated conspiracy to smuggle this baby back into the country?'

But when he looked into it, he realized that documents were easy to falsify.

'I grew up with Wall Street geniuses. What they do in terms of fraud and how they change documents,' he said.

He told *Fox Nation* that he had just got himself a new birth certificate. So where was Obama's?

'People have birth certificates,' he said. 'He doesn't have a birth certificate. He may have one but there's something on that, maybe religion, maybe it says he is a Muslim. I don't know. Maybe he doesn't want that. Or he may not have one. But I will tell you this. If he wasn't born in this country, it's one of the great scams of all time.'

On 27 April 2011, when The Donald heard that the state of Hawaii had finally released the president's official birth certificate, ever modest, he was prepared to take full credit for it.

'Today I'm very proud of myself, because I've accomplished something that nobody else has been able to accomplish,' he said at an impromptu press conference. 'I was just informed, while on the helicopter, that our president has finally released a birth certificate. I want to look at it, but I hope it's true, so that we can get on to much more important matters, so the press can stop asking me questions.... But I am really honoured, frankly, to have played such a big role in hopefully, hopefully getting rid of this issue. Now, we have to look at it, we have to see, is it real? Is it proper? What's on it? But I hope it checks out beautifully. I am really proud, I am really honoured.'

◆

President Obama expressed his relief that the matter had been put to rest at the 2011 White House Correspondents' Dinner by mercilessly roasting an unamused Trump.

'No one is happier – no one is prouder – to put this birth certificate matter to rest than The Donald,' Obama said. 'And that's because he can finally get back to focusing on the issues that matter: Like, did we fake the moon landing? What really happened in Roswell? And where are Biggie and Tupac?'

He continued: 'All kidding aside, obviously we all know about your credentials and breadth of experience. For example ... no, seriously, just recently, in an episode of *Celebrity Apprentice* at the steakhouse, the men's cooking team did not impress the judges from Omaha Steaks. And there was a lot of blame to go around, but you, Mr Trump, recognized that the real problem was a lack of leadership, and so ultimately you didn't blame Li'l Jon or Meat Loaf – you fired Gary Busey. And these are the kinds of decisions that would keep me up at night. Well handled, sir. Well handled. Say what you will about Mr Trump, he certainly would bring some change to the White House.'

◆

But The Donald was not going to take this lying down. His suspicions were piqued that Obama was not even a Christian! On 28 December 2011, he tweeted: 'What a convenient mistake: @BarackObama issued a statement for Kwanza [sic] but failed to issue one for Christmas.'

Kwanzaa is a week-long celebration of the African heritage of African Americans, starting on 26 December and first celebrated in 1966. At last, the smoking gun.

Then on 6 August 2012, he tweeted: 'An "extremely credible source" has called my office and told me that @BarackObama's birth certificate is a fraud.'

◆

Unfortunately the 'extremely credible source' never came forward. Giving the keynote speech at the Washington National Press Club on 27 May 2014, he was asked if he regretted questioning Obama's eligibility.

'Not even a little bit. I don't regret it. Why would I regret it?' he said, adding that 'there's a very big chance' Obama was born in America.

◆

Asked about it again on *Meet The Press* in September 2015, he told host Chuck Todd: 'I just don't discuss it. Really, it hasn't been brought up in a long time.'

But then The Donald had been having a battle with 'the

loser' Todd for some time. On 23 January 2015, he tweeted: 'Word is that @NBCNews is firing sleepy eyes Chuck Todd in that his ratings on *Meet the Press* are setting record lows. He's a real loser.' He also called NBC News 'the Obama network', then said: 'Can't wait to see #SleepyEyes on the next #CelebrityApprentice. Oh wait, he would have to be a celeb.'

Two days later, Donald was suggesting that he replace Todd on *Meet the Press*.

'I am convinced that sleepy eyes Chuck Todd was only a placeholder for someone else at *Meet the Press*. He bombed, franchise in ruins!' he tweeted on 27 January.

Then minutes later, he tweeted: '*Apprentice*=big hit. *Miss Universe*=Big hit. I always get ratings. If I hosted *Meet the Press* instead of Sleepy Eyes, a smash!'

Seven minutes after that, Donald was at it again: 'So many people have told me that I should host *Meet the Press* and replace the moron who is on now. Just too busy, especially the next 10 years!'

The problem was that Todd's ratings were actually climbing. Nevertheless, the antagonism continued. On 6 December Todd presented a segment contrasting what Trump had said previously with what he was saying then – for example, he had once said: 'Hillary Clinton, I think, is a terrific woman', while he was now saying: 'I think Hillary would be a terrible president.

That evening Donald responded in typically robust style.

'Sleep eyes @ChuckTodd is killing *Meet The Press*. Isn't he pathetic? Love watching him fail!' he tweeted, and: 'I hear that sleepy eyes @chucktodd will be fired like a dog from ratings starved *Meet The Press*? I can't imagine what is taking so long!'

'You know who started the birther movement?' The Donald asked CNN's Wolf Blitzer on 4 May 2016. 'You know who started it? Do you know who questioned his birth certificate, one of the first? Hillary Clinton. She's the one that started it. She brought it up years before it was brought up by me.'

The Washington Post's Fact Checker gave The Donald's claim a rating of four Pinocchios – the maximum. One Pinocchio stands for minor shading of the facts and four means outright lies.

Nevertheless, with Obama, The Donald was willing to let bygones be bygones. When he announced his candidacy in 2015, he said: 'Remember, Obamacare really kicks in. In '16. 2016. Obama's gonna be out playing golf. He might even be on one of my courses. I would invite him, I actually would say it. I have the best courses in the world, so I'd say, you know what, if he wants to. I have one right next to the White House. Right on the Potomac. If he'd like to play, that's fine. In fact, I'd love him to leave early and play.'

He had extended a similar invitation to Bill Clinton, even though The Donald had tweeted that Bill had 'demonstrated a penchant for sexism'. But the Winged Foot Golf Club, where Donald was a member, was so exclusive it had a fifteen-year waiting list.

'It wouldn't have been tough for him to get in, but for the scandals. . . . He's not going to get in,' he told the *Orlando Sentinel* in January 2000 when Bill was still president. However, The Donald was prepared to be magnanimous.

'I'm building a beautiful golf club five minutes from his home, and I would be happy to have him as a member,' he said.

———◆———

He even managed to insult the office he was running for.

'I've given up a tremendous amount to run for president,' The Donald told Wolf Blitzer. 'I gave up two more seasons of *Celebrity Apprentice*.'

He should have stuck with it. The pay's better.

Epilogue

'Anyone who thinks my story is anywhere near over is sadly mistaken.'

So spake The Donald. And that was in 1997.